CYBERSECURITY AND CYBERWAR IN 2021 FOR BEGINNERS

Network Topologies, Protocols, And Strategies. Measures to Secure Your Cyber Networks

By William Richards

Copyright © 2020 William Richards

All rights reserved.

No part of this guide may be reproduced in any form without permission in writing from the publisher except in the case of brief quotations embodied in critical articles or reviews.

Legal & Disclaimer

The information contained in this book and its contents is not designed to replace or take the place of any form of medical or professional advice; and is not meant to replace the need for independent medical, financial, legal or other professional advice or services, as may be required. The content and information in this book have been provided for educational and entertainment purposes only.

The content and information contained in this book has been compiled from sources deemed reliable, and it is accurate to the best of the Author's knowledge, information and belief. However, the Author cannot guarantee its accuracy and validity and cannot be held liable for any errors and/or omissions. Further, changes are periodically made to this book as and when needed. Where appropriate and/or necessary, you must consult a professional (including but not limited to your doctor, attorney, financial advisor or such other professional advisor) before using any of the suggested remedies, techniques, or information in this book.

Upon using the contents and information contained in this book, you agree to hold harmless the Author from and against any damages, costs, and expenses, including any legal fees potentially resulting from the application of any of the information provided by this book. This disclaimer applies to any loss, damages or injury caused by the use and application, whether directly or indirectly, of any advice or information presented, whether for breach of contract, tort, negligence, personal injury, criminal intent, or under any other cause of action.

You agree to accept all risks of using the information presented inside this book.

You agree that by continuing to read this book, where appropriate and/or necessary, you shall consult a professional (including but not limited to your doctor, attorney, or financial advisor or such other advisor as needed) before using any of the suggested remedies, techniques, or information in this book.

TABLE OF CONTENTS

INTRODUCTION TO CYBERSECURITY — 6

THE 3 MOST SERIOUS CYBER ATTACKS — 8
IT SECURITY, DATA PROTECTION AND PRIVACY — 14
IT SECURITY, HOW TO DO IT IN THE COMPANY — 15
IT SECURITY: THE ROLE OF CYBERSECURITY AND SYSTEM INTEGRATORS — 16
2020 A NEGATIVE START FOR IT SECURITY — 17

PROBLEMS ARISING IN THE INDUSTRY — 20

TIPS FOR MORE SECURITY: HOW TO STOP DATA THEFT — 22
EFFECTIVE METHODS FOR SAFE SURFING — 25
TAKE THE FOLLOWING PRECAUTIONS WHEN WORKING REMOTELY: — 34
THE UNITED STATES IS UNDER CYBER ATTACK — 39
CYBERCRIME IS MORE OF A CONCERN TO AMERICANS THAN DRUGS AND MONEY LAUNDERING — 41

DETRIMENTAL DATA BREACHES — 47

UNDERSTANDING AND PREVENTING RISK — 53

SMALL CYBERCRIME EVENTS — 56

HOW NOT TO GET EASILY HACKED? — 62

LEARN TO RECOGNIZE SUSPICIOUS BEHAVIOR — 63
5 MORE TRICKS TO AVOID BEING HACKED — 72

CYBERSECURITY IN THE 2000'S V 2020. — 76

2010: IRANIAN NUCLEAR INFRASTRUCTURE 77
2013: TARGET 78
2014: SONY 78
2017: NOTPETYA 79
2017: EQUIFAX 80
2018: MARRIOTT 81
THE IMPACT OF CYBERSECURITY ON THE ECONOMY AND DEMOCRACY OF THE COUNTRY: THE ROLE OF SCIENTIFIC RESEARCH 81
DEMOCRACY 87
FINANCE 87
TRANSPORTATION 89
INDUSTRY 90
COMMUNICATION AND PRESS 91

LEADERS IN CYBERSECURITY **114**

LEADING COMPANIES IN CYBERSECURITY **127**

THE 10 BEST ACQUISITIONS OF CYBERSECURITY COMPANIES 135
    Amazon 136
    Cisco 136
    Claroty 137
    Darktrace 138
    Intel 138
    McAfee 139
    Oracle 140
    Palo Alto Networks 140
    Proofpoint 140
    Red Hat 141

GLOBAL CYBERSECURITY COOPERATION **156**

THE NEW CRIMINAL SCENARIOS	172
CYBERCRIME AS A NEW FACE OF ORGANIZED CRIME	190

THE FUTURE OF CYBERSECURITY — 199

PUBLIC WI-FI WILL CONTINUE TO BE DANGEROUS	205
THE CYBER RISKS TO BE ADDRESSED IN 2020	217

CYBERSECURITY AND CYBERWAR
IN 2021

INTRODUCTION TO CYBERSECURITY

Why does everyone talk about cybersecurity?

How should people and companies implement it?

These are some questions addressed in this book.

CYBERSECURITY AND CYBERWAR
IN 2021

Cybercrime, hacker attacks, ransomware, WannaCry ….

Unfortunately, we have learned to familiarize ourselves, often at our expense, with IT security, also known as Cybersecurity. An issue that, precisely due to the multiplication of attacks from the outside, is becoming crucial for companies of any sector and size. But what exactly is cybersecurity? What are the affected areas and what are the rules to follow in order to have a good protection of company information systems (always bearing in mind that zero risk can never exist)?

Four in five victims of a hacker attack do not realize they have been hit within the first week of the event.

Lack of cybersecurity could cost $6 trillion by 2021 - this is an estimate of the annual global damage caused by cybercrime alone. Yet four in five victims of a hacker attack that penetrates their IT infrastructure do not realize they were hit within the first week of the event. So reveals Verizon, the largest wireless telecommunications provider in the United States. But the truth is that much more often this time stretches up to 300 days. Microsoft itself claims that an attacker manages to remain dormant on a compromised system for up to 200 days.

These are just some striking data of a global scenario in which cybercrime targets individuals, small and large companies, critical public infrastructures (hospitals and airports, for example) and nation states. And it grows in volume and effectiveness every year, thus driving the increase in the cybersecurity offer and the profits of some big names in the sector.

Rising costs of cybercrime and cyber attacks

At risk is a lot of money, geopolitical balance and power. It is no coincidence that Vladimir Putin stated long ago that the leading nation in the field of artificial intelligence will be the one capable of ruling the world. Already today Russia, together with Ukraine, Macedonia, Albania, Bulgaria and Romania, develop excellent hackers.

THE 3 MOST SERIOUS CYBER ATTACKS

MAY 12, 2017 - The day of WannaCry, which is a ransomware responsible for a large-scale epidemic involving computers with outdated versions of Microsoft's operating system, Windows.

A virus that encrypted the files of the affected machines and demanded a ransom of several hundred dollars to return them to the owner. 230,000 computers infected. Affected companies (Portugal Telecom, Deutsche Bahn,

FedEx, Telefónica, Iberdrola, Gas Natural, Tuenti, Renault) and public bodies (the Russian Ministry of the Interior, the University of Milan-Bicocca, numerous hospitals in the United Kingdom) in 150 countries.

JUNE 27, 2017 - Another ransomware fault. Its name, Petya, initially remained imprinted in the memory - not just digital - of Ukrainian banks and companies (with repercussions on the Chernobyl nuclear power plant). And then, thanks to the network, in the world.

Infected were the British advertising agency Wpp, the French building materials company Saint Gobain, the pharmaceutical company Merck Sharp & Dome, the shipping giant Moller- Maersk. For the latter, a 12-day stop of activities that cost it about 300 million dollars in damage and a collapse of the share price. Part of the management resigned following the incident.

7 SEPTEMBER 2017 - A horrible date for Equifax and its customers. The company, one of the three largest companies in the world in the collection and evaluation of credit information for individuals and businesses, claims to have suffered a data breach on 143 of its 800 million users. Most of the loan or credit card concessions in the US passes through Equifax.

The incident forced CEO Richard Smith to leave office and produced an FBI investigation. Three top managers of the company would sell 2 million Equifax shares before the cyber intrusion was revealed and the stock collapsed.

CYBERSECURITY AND CYBERWAR IN 2021

Not surprisingly, the new international legislation on privacy (General Data Protection Regulation, GDPR) came into force on May 25, for all companies operating on the continent, provides 72-hour time limit for notifying the attacks from when you realize you have suffered them. With very high penalties in case of tampering: up to 4% of turnover.

What is Cyber security?

As always, it is useful to start with the definitions. The first definition is that relating to information security which is characterized by "safeguarding the confidentiality, integrity and availability of information managed by an organization". More specifically, IT security, which is a subset of information security, is aimed at protecting IT equipment from voluntary attack actions, and which can be defined as the set of products, services, organizational rules and individual behaviors that protect systems and computer scientists of a company.

The many different areas of Cyber security:

As it is easy to understand, computer security actually concerns many distinct activities: you can have security at the application level, at the data level, at the network level and so on. So much so that according to a very recent Gartner analysis, in 2018 approximately 114 billion dollars will be spent on cybersecurity globally: over half, that is almost 59 billion dollars, are the prerogative of connected services. The second item of expenditure is represented by products that deal with the protection of infrastructures, which absorb just over 14 billion. Network protection, on the other hand, has an impact of almost 12.5 billion. Less important than what one might think is the consumer world: the software purchased by ordinary users produce a turnover of just under 6.5 billion, destined to grow slightly in 2019. Identity and Access management, also crucial in the corporate environment, has a turnover of a slightly higher segment which will develop to be significantly higher: from a value of 8.8 billion in 2017 to 9.7 billion in 2018, which will become 10.6 in 2019. Still a minority, but in double-digit growth, are areas such as Application security and Data Security.

A little history of cyber attacks

But what are you defending against? It should be noted that information security has a thirty-year history: in 1986 from Pakistan arrived the first computer virus in history, Brain A. Then it became AIDS in 1989, a malware that had very strong similarities with current ransomware. From then on, each year has had its own particular viruses: 1992 saw the arrival of Michelangelo, 1995 of Concept, while the millennium ended with Happy 99 (which can be defined as the first malware of the web era). Going forward over the years we come to more recent names such as Zeus and Stuxnet: the latter can be considered as a real watershed in the history of malware, because it has proved capable of affecting not only the Windows environment but also systems of automation.

Malware is increasingly the king of attacks

Currently, however, the majority of attacks are carried out using methods now named millions of times by operators in the sector.

According to the latest Clusit report in 2017, serious attacks were carried out in the majority of cases (68%) with trivial techniques, such as SQLi, DDoS, known vulnerabilities, Phishing, a "simple" malware, is a growing trend by 12 percentage points compared to 2016.

The costs of this complex of activities, as it is easy to imagine, are considerable: the Clusit estimate is that cybercrime alone caused damages of 500 billion dollars in 2017.

Scams, extortion, theft of money and personal data have hit almost a billion people in the world, causing private citizens alone an estimated loss of 180 billion dollars. As for the bill (even if referring to 2016) it is equally high: it is assumed for almost 10 billion dollars, that is a value ten times higher than that of the current national investments in information security which, as previously mentioned, amount about a billion dollars.

Ransomware, what it is and how it defends itself

The most famous variant of the vast family of ransomware was that of cryptolockers. Here we also discovered some ways to recover files from infected devices.

Then there are some basic rules that allow you to limit the possibility of falling into the traps of ransomware which, basically, translate into the need to keep your guard up. First of all, it is necessary to frequently update applications and software (malware such as ransomware, in fact, exploit the security flaws present in obsolete software), as well as use a good antivirus. Great care should be taken when using email (not opening suspicious attachments or links). More generally, making regular backups should always be the best practice, because in this way the blackmail weapon available to cybercriminals is cut at the root.

Cyber security: problems come from within

But why do cybercriminals manage to successfully end their attacks so often? It is not only a problem of poor defenses in place but also of breaches that attackers can count on. This very often coincides with corporate employees: according to a recent survey by Kaspersky Lab and B2B International, the lack of awareness related to cybersecurity is still alarming in companies around the world. The study, which involved 7,993 employees, found that only one in ten employees (12%) is fully aware of the security policies and rules established by the company they work for.

Not only that: as many as 24% of the believe that their company has not established any policy. Yet, according to another Kaspersky research, inattentive staff contributed to cybersecurity incidents in 46% of cases over the past year. Almost half of the interviewees (49%) think, in fact, that all employees - including themselves - should take responsibility for protecting company resources from cyber threats.

Given these premises, employees not only run the risk of becoming victims of cybercriminals themselves but also risk making their company victims of cyber threats. Small and medium-sized businesses should also benefit from regular training on the importance of cybersecurity for staff and customized solutions.

IT SECURITY, DATA PROTECTION AND PRIVACY

All this changes the security perspective: the owner is made responsible (the so-called accountability), asking him to evaluate in its context and in relation to its risks, which are the most adequate security measures to guarantee data protection. In this sense, another fundamental element introduced is the request to carry out an assessment of the risks to which the information is subject, with different degrees of complexity depending on the organization. In essence, it forces all those who have to do with citizens' data to deal with security and to think from a risk management perspective, that is an attitude that until now was the prerogative only of large companies (and not all in reality).

IT SECURITY, HOW TO DO IT IN THE COMPANY

While there is no doubt that the management of IT security differs according to the size of the company, it is still possible to outline some basic principles that help to understand how one can defend oneself effectively. A good security policy consists of at least five successive phases:

- identification: it is necessary to understand which assets are to be protected and from which threats,

- the provision of adequate protection measures: security checks and countermeasures, for example by installing firewalls,

- the negative event detection

- the response - the reaction that trigger the defenses to limit the damage caused by the attack

- and, finally, the ability to recover, to restore the original conditions - disaster recovery

More generally, one of the first things to put in place is to develop an internal culture: it is useless to install bombastic security measures if your staff continues to click on whatever they receive by email. Secondly, it serves an approach geared to the risks, which will serve to calibrate the choices, depending also on the present budget. With a good active prevention system and regular scans, it is then possible to minimize the data loss. It is very important to make a regular backup, which allows continuity of access to information, which represents a fundamental dimension of cybersecurity.

IT SECURITY: THE ROLE OF CYBERSECURITY AND SYSTEM INTEGRATORS

How can cybersecurity address the world of security? We need to start from the basics: cybersecurity is increasingly a strategic priority for every company. What has really changed is the business model with which companies operate, which makes a leap in quality inevitable on the part of security specialists, who must be able to guarantee the necessary support to their customers and create added value for their own customers, mixing it with the right degree of innovation. Also, because, in addition to hacker attacks, companies must guard against the excessive crowding of the security world, which has about 2000 companies on the market. Security consultants therefore have the difficult task of selecting the most suitable ones for each specific business need, making the necessary integration of technologies and platforms as simple as possible.

Beyond training in the classroom and in the laboratory, however, a security professional must have a primarily practical perspective on the problems. In recent years, the demand for security professionals has clearly increased. Indeed, the demand is greater than the availability of these figures, also thanks to the greater exposure favored by cases like that of WannaCry. Furthermore, the increased dependence of companies on information systems makes it the most critical issue in itself. All this is making this profession attractive from an economic point of view, even if cybersecurity experts are rarely employed on an ongoing basis by companies, mostly finding themselves working as a freelance.

2020 A NEGATIVE START FOR IT SECURITY

Despite the increased overall attention to the issue of cyber security, cybercrime attacks show no sign of abating, quite the contrary. This is a point out by a study by Clusit, relating to the first half of 2020: in this period, 730 serious attacks were recorded globally, corresponding to a growth of 31% compared to the previous half year. Numbers that make the first half of 2020 the worst ever. Most of these cybercrime incursions are not particularly elaborate and sophisticated: "Simple Malware" - industrially produced at ever decreasing costs - is confirmed as the most used attack vector (40% of the total attacks).

CYBERSECURITY AND CYBERWAR IN 2021

Windows 7: End of support opens security issue

An additional problem for cybersecurity is represented by the upcoming end of free support for Windows 7, scheduled for January 14, 2020, which will therefore leave companies and users without the protection of security patches. All companies that do not update their OS remain EXPOSED to many families of malware and attacks of various kinds. A problem that is destined to be devastating due to the presence of obsolete applications that are used in the old OS, which in turn can be used by cybercriminals to carry out further attacks. However, a real upgrade race does not seem foreseeable at the moment, due to the presence of economic and technical obstacles.

Cyberwar: Russia also under attack

One of the hottest areas of cyber security is undoubtedly that relating to Cyberwar: groups of hackers, specially backed and financed by sovereign states, who carry out attacks with the aim of stealing data or damaging the functioning of organizations, either public or private, of powers considered rivals. Russia has often been accused of pushing such practices, but in July 2019 Moscow was the victim of a cyberwar attack. In particular SyTech, supplier of the secret service Fsb (Federal Security Service of the Russian Federation), was the victim of a cyberattack: cyber criminals (under the pseudonym of "0v1ru $) allegedly stole - according to what the BBC reconstructed - about 75 terabytes of confidential information. Cybercriminals later shared the stolen information to the hacker collective Digital Revolution, which sent it to some news outlets.

Cyber security in 2020: the industrialization of cybercrime continues

The 2020 edition of the Clusit report confirmed the growing trend of cyber-attacks. Globally, in fact, the study highlights how 1,670 serious attacks were recorded in 2019, or 7% more than in 2018. Another phenomenon highlighted by the Clusit report is the growing industrialization of cybercrime: cybercriminals appear more framed in real organizations that conduct operations on an ever-increasing scale, with an "industrial" logic, regardless of both territorial constraints and the type of targets, aiming only to maximize the economic result: not surprisingly 24% of the total attacks surveyed can be classified as "Multiple Targets". The Clusit Report notes that the industrialization of cybercrime leads to favoring the use of "simple" vectors, which can be easily assembled in numerous variants: in particular, cybercriminals in 2019 launched attacks using malware in 44% of cases (+ 24.8% compared to last year).

CYBERSECURITY AND CYBERWAR IN 2021

PROBLEMS ARISING IN THE INDUSTRY

Cyber security: protect yourself better while surfing the Internet

With the increase in interconnection in the digital world, the issue of security is becoming increasingly important. The password is critical for cyber security. In fact, on the Internet there are always new dangers that represent a threat for companies, but also for individuals which can sometimes cause enormous damage. The topic of information security is therefore as topical as never before, but it does not only concern Internet security, but also deals with all other aspects and sectors of Information Technology.

To ensure the safety of a user on the network, there are many means available ranging from explaining the dangers present on the network, participating in specific courses for Internet safety, up to the use of tools and programs with which users can protect against attacks in cyber space.

Considering that illegal actions do not take place only via the Internet, the subject of cybersecurity includes yet another aspect, namely the protection from the dangers that exploit modern electronic options, in the field of telecommunications.

The dangers of the digital world

The concept of cybercrime is very broad and this refers to online crime. All those security measures implemented on the Internet are often associated with it in the common imagination, forgetting however that within the concept of cyber-crime other forms of crime can be classified, such as that relating to electronic means, telecommunications. For this reason, the term cybercrime is also used to summarize all these concepts.

Cyber-crime also includes the improper use of private and personal as well as sensitive information stolen via the Internet from a corporate network or, with the help of ad hoc tools, from a person's credit card. Phishing, ghost travel and identity theft via social networks are among the cybercrimes. More generally, all criminal actions aimed at improper use of user data are part of the acts committed by cyber criminals, but DDoS attacks and the spread of malware, which equally pursue illegal purposes, should not be forgotten.

What is cyber security and how is it guaranteed?

The vastness of the topic and the current degree of danger, especially caused by the increasing possibilities that the digital world offers day after day, already show how cyber security is very important. Just think of how much data is processed daily on your computer, tablet or smartphone, how many accounts are used on the Internet for the different applications, on the many platforms and how much bank data and other sensitive information are requested in everyday life. All this data is interceptable and at the mercy of cyber criminals who exploit it for their illicit purposes.

Most consumers will have at least once dealt with misuse of their credit card. But if you don't take the right precautions you risk running into far more serious consequences. To prevent cybercriminals from harming a person, and therefore resulting in legal consequences for the victim, it is important to take an active interest in the topic, and find out about the necessary security measures and the tools available for IT security, both by the individual or other people close to the victim or in the case of corporations, their own company.

T**IPS FOR MORE SECURITY: HOW TO STOP DATA THEFT**

Buying simple gadgets, like an aluminum card holder, prevents offline data theft. In fact, using this small but effective stratagem the extortion of credit card data or other sensitive bank data by criminals is prevented, or at least made difficult.

Broadly speaking, a similar barrier can also be erected for computer systems; the very important use of secure passwords. While they may appear long, unintuitive, and hard to remember, they are very effective in terms of basic protection. In fact, choosing a good password serves to prevent a person from gaining access to a computer unduly and prevents the user's attempt from being mistakenly successful, when a password is entered.

But for complete basic protection, other IT security tools are also essential, which should become a standard for all users. For example, a firewall is essential: it can be present on the computer and / or router. In fact, a firewall serves to prevent unauthorized access to your computer or network. From the settings you can configure who or what can access the Internet from the network and vice versa.

A firewall is particularly effective when combined with an antivirus program that not only detects viruses, Trojans and other malware, but also manages to eliminate them or resolve the situation quickly. Furthermore, regularly scanning your PC or network for cyber threats is good practice and should be part of the practices to be used to ensure the cyber security of your system.

The current risk situation

While it's not often that you are the victim of a digital attack, you shouldn't lose sight of the overall situation. Individuals, companies, entire economic sectors, institutions and governments are all potential targets for cybercrime or have been in the past.

At the end of 2015 a book by the National Cyber Security Laboratory, which shed light on the situation of growing threats and preparations for cybernetic and the defense mechanisms that will meet the new security requirements. In fact, the digital evolution brings with it new tools, but also the increase of old and new threats that undermine the security of systems.

Thus, it emerges that in the business and political world there is still no managerial awareness of the importance of IT security. It is also underlined that at the time of writing this report, the first steps in the area of cyber security were only beginning to be taken, and how this entailed a delay in the clear delineation of a well-defined digital strategy.

Defend yourself from cyber attacks

The goal is therefore to create an environment throughout the territory that is more resistant to cyber-attacks, but also to provide solutions to protect the critical infrastructures of the administration, enhance the solutions of the private sector, improve the awareness of citizens and companies in regards to cyber dangers, as well as consolidating collaborative relationships with other international organizations, which perform a similar function.

Within this organization, the "cyberchallenge" initiative was also launched, which aims to train children from middle school and the first years of university to introduce them to professions in the field of information security. In fact, the task of this Committee is also to create local and national training plans.

It is hoped that small companies will also be aware of this issue and that the risks associated with these cyber threats will be reduced.

EFFECTIVE METHODS FOR SAFE SURFING

It is essential to always be up-to-date to ensure IT security in the private and business sectors. In addition to the use of special tools for computer security, you can rely on effective tips, tricks and methods that have established themselves over the years.

It starts with keeping all systems up to date. Both the integral operating system and all applications, regardless of whether it is a desktop computer, a notebook, a tablet or a smartphone, should all always have the latest version. In fact, previous programs represent a vulnerability that can be exploited by cyber criminals.

Antivirus programs and a well configured firewall are indispensable, a solid foundation on which the company network and PCs should be built. Despite the increasingly complex threats circulating, the latest versions are able to protect against daily dangers and prevent greater damage from being caused. As important as firewalls and anti-virus software are, it is also essential to control the permissions to access and write data. In addition, companies must take into account the risks associated with social engineering. In the past, criminals deceived information from large companies by pretending to be cybersecurity employees who needed another employee's login data to do the job for them. It is essential to verify which user was active at a given moment and thus trace his activities.

It is therefore an absolute priority to raise awareness among workers of similar practices and strengthen their awareness of data processing with appropriate courses. Courses should be offered for workers to inform about guidelines governing the use of the corporate network and the devices connected to it.

Companies and institutions must not fail to regularly inform themselves through official sources, to stay up to date on new threats and the consequent measures to protect themselves and prevent the advance of the threat. Instead, private individuals can stay up to date on specialized portals, as well as on the pages of security software manufacturers, who regularly release updates and patches to ensure the functions of the programs and expand them.

It quickly becomes clear that cybersecurity is never easy to guarantee. No matter how scrupulously security measures are put in place on the Internet and in other areas of the digital environment, there will always be security holes and vulnerabilities. In fact, even cyber criminals work tirelessly to develop new methods or improve existing ones to steal data or sabotage systems. In the worst case, financial damage or personal injury is caused. Although the fight against cybercrime may seem hopeless, privately but also in the workplace, precautions must be taken to make attacks by hackers and cyber criminals as difficult as possible. It's common knowledge that no one would ever think of giving house keys to a thief ...

Protecting company information and data is the duty of anyone who works there, even of personnel not directly involved in the process of "securing" the infrastructure. A company that invests in the most sophisticated technological means in terms of cybersecurity could in fact be compromised by the carelessness of an employee who, to go to the bathroom, leaves his desk unattended - on which papers and documents of vital importance for the company are perhaps laid. Sometimes a second of inattention or a click on a wrong link is enough to jeopardize the entire IT network of a company.

Every employee must be aware of playing a fundamental role in the very survival of the company and must therefore take into account a series of precautions to avoid insecure actions, likely to spread sensitive information to ill-intentioned individuals. In this sense, an employer who invests time and energy in educating their employees on how to secure their electronic devices is a forward-thinking leader who knows how to minimize the possibility of cyber-attacks on their company: knowledge is power.

CYBERSECURITY AND CYBERWAR IN 2021

Some rules that it's very, very important for the employees of any company - whether small or large - to absolutely ensure are followed when carrying out their work:

- Keep your operating system, browser, and antivirus program updated: cyber scammers are always finding new ways to bypass a company's security mechanisms. For this reason, downloading the latest versions of anti-virus systems and keeping the operating system and browser updated to the latest versions is a necessary - but not sufficient - condition if you want to avoid the terrible consequences of a cyber-attack. Hence, every employee must promptly install security software updates (both on company devices and on personal devices used at work) when the company sends instructions and directives in this regard.

- Use strong passwords and multi-factor authentication systems: using strong passwords is one of the most effective methods to avoid threats to a company's cybersecurity.

A secure password contains at least 10/12 characters (including numbers, special characters, combinations of upper- and lower-case letters), does not include personal information (such as the name, telephone number, date of birth of a family member); You should definitely avoid using the same login and password combination for multiple systems, as well as using the browser's autofill feature for passwords. The use of password management software is highly recommended.

Training to recognize phishing:

All employees must know how to recognize - and therefore prevent - the phenomenon of phishing. Cyber crooks - appearing as credible and reliable subjects - can extract vital information from the employee of the company he works for through fictitious e-mails that often contain links that - once clicked - lead the victim to share sensitive company data.

Given these threats, employees should adhere to a number of phishing best practices:

- Do not share sensitive information via email;

- Pay attention to URLs on a website - many phishing attacks are conducted via malicious websites that mimic legitimate ones;

- Check for suspicious emails: if in doubt, contact the cybersecurity department;

Keep a tidy desk:

- although it may seem trivial, the employees of a company do not always respect this simple trick. Yet, keeping your work plan in order is essential to avoid problems (such as theft and loss). A tidy desk facilitates us in checking what we have in plain sight and above all allows us to understand if something is missing. Theft of documents on cluttered desks can be discovered only months later.

Here is a list of the bad habits that employees often develop in the workplace:

- ❖ Leave a PC without screen lock protection / password: it is necessary to ensure that access to the device is blocked when the employee is not present
- ❖ Leave sensitive documents unattended on the desk: it is essential to store them in a safe and inaccessible place
- ❖ Not closing files / archives: this makes their content accessible to anyone (including those with bad intentions) and they should always be locked away
- ❖ Leaving cell phones and USB devices without setting password protection
- ❖ Leaving confidential and sensitive notes / information on whiteboards
- ❖ Writing down usernames, passwords or various security codes on post-its or other pieces of accessible paper
- ❖ Leaving the key of a closed drawer lying around

❖ View calendars in full screen: in this way, everyone can read their content (calendars often also contain information on customers and products)

Destroy documents containing confidential information:

- it is of fundamental importance to avoid crumpling confidential documents and then throwing them in the trash. One of the favorite methods of cyber criminals to steal confidential information is Dumpster Diving, which literally means Diving into the garbage. Whenever we need to dispose of a document, make sure to destroy it properly so that the information it contains is no longer available. Every office should have a paper shredder! The same concept applies to electronic devices, such as USB keys or portable disks.

Protect your data:

- as a person does in private life, an employee must absolutely avoid sharing security codes, sensitive data and vital company information with third parties, bearing in mind that often scammers using social engineering techniques can make requests that apparently, seeming legitimate, conceal their criminal intent. Any employee must refrain from sharing and disseminating information regarding their company and must adopt mechanisms for encrypting confidential data.

Do not let confidential documents leave your company:

- it is essential that all confidential documents circulate as little as possible and, above all, do not leave the company unless exceptional conditions exist. The same applies to information recorded on electronic devices:

- ❖ Do not send emails containing confidential documents
- ❖ Do not store confidential documents on Dropbox, Google Drive etc.
- ❖ Do not store confidential documents on your personal devices.

Protect your devices:

The main vulnerabilities in terms of IT security are linked to the loss by workers of their electronic devices (think of the fact that a laptop is stolen every 53 seconds at airports). Given the impossibility of predicting such situations, it is good for the employees of a company to adopt a series of precautions. In this regard, it is essential to activate the tracking functions of your phone / tablet / PC so as to easily find the device in case of loss; furthermore, it is essential to use a passcode or a biometric authorization (e.g. fingerprint, facial recognition) to make access to one's electronic devices more secure; it is also advisable to keep electronic devices "clean", using antivirus and anti-malware.

Finally, it is of significant importance to use the safest method to block the screens of the various devices available, as well as to consider encrypting sensitive data.

Recognize social engineering:

Every web user adopts a series of behaviors on the Internet, some of which risk compromising their safety both from a personal point of view and from a work point of view.

For example, some details we have described on our personal blog (such as our dog's name) could be used by third parties to access our personal data (think about security questions). It is essential to know the techniques used by social engineers to steal sensitive information.

Do not use uncontrolled USB devices

All USB devices must be treated as if they contain malware. Consequently, it is advisable not to insert any similar device into a computer used to access company data and information or allow others to do so (even if they are known people);

Enable Windows in the "Show filename extensions" option:

Some extensions (.Exe, .doc, .Xls, .Js etc ...) are potentially harmful and recognizing them can allow us to avoid a cyber-attack.

Do not allow Office macros to run:

Office macros can contain malicious code. It is essential to disable and enable them only when we are sure of the source of the macro.

Remotely connecting to the office from a secured Wi-Fi network:

Unsecured Wi-Fi networks make information traffic potentially accessible, so easy for a criminal to access the communication to steal confidential information. The same goes for when we have to connect to sites that require the use of confidential information such as credit card codes or access to your online bank. In these cases, it is absolutely necessary to avoid being connected to an unsecured Wi-Fi network.

TAKE THE FOLLOWING PRECAUTIONS WHEN WORKING REMOTELY:

- Do not access confidential information from public devices;

- Use the computer so that no one can see the screen (eg. Back facing against the wall): the main social engineering techniques include " Shoulder Surfing", a device aimed at stealing sensitive information and data (eg PIN, password ...) spying on the victim. It is good to remember how the technique can be implemented either up close (the scammer is physically close to the victim) or from a distance (through cameras or similar tools);

- Perform a full logout once you want to end your work session

- Deselect the option to store browser login information

- Permanently delete every downloaded file

- If possible, use the private browsing function

- Enable firewall protection both at work and at home. This is fundamental protection that prevents unauthorized users from accessing a system's resources. It would also be better not to be satisfied with corporate firewall protection but to install your own at home;

- Surf the Internet safely: in this regard, it is possible to mention a series of best practices for employees:

- Be careful with online downloads

- Only browse websites with proven reliability

- Be careful of what website you are browsing; ensure you are accessing the original one and not a fake one. Always monitor the URL being accessed.

- Make sure that the website on which delicate operations such as purchases or transfers are carried out uses the Https protocol, which allows you to encrypt - making it more secure - the sender / recipient communication

- When you receive a mail which includes a link that you don't know, never click on the links but manually enter the destination address on the browser navigation bar

- Use social media wisely and protect your personal information that others can see

Back up your files: This should be done regularly and is an essential part of preventing damage done by cyber security attacks. In this case it is good to follow the rules and procedures that all company's must have developed in this regard. Backup is a fundamental tool especially in the case of threats to sensitive data: think of ransomware, a malware capable of infecting a computer system, which compromises access to the user, who then asks for a ransom in exchange for restoring the initial conditions. Performing a regular backup process - and therefore a copy - of personal data (including documents, photos …) on a hard disk connected via USB (physical backup) or on a cloud is an excellent solution to stem similar security problems;

Do not work on your PC with administrative rights: in the event of a malware infection the effects could be devastating. Using a user profile with restricted privileges will contain the malware in a limited perimeter.

Talk to your IT department: a friendly and constant relationship with the company's IT department is essential both if you want to prevent a problem and if you want to correct it. It is therefore good that any suspicious activity as well as any warning of the security software is immediately reported to IT experts.

In particular, the IT department must always be aware of:

- ✓ An unexpected increase in pop-up and spam ads
- ✓ A noticeable drop in performance
- ✓ Frequent error messages
- ✓ A new homepage or a new default search engine
- ✓ Reporting of the presence of a malware by antivirus / anti-malware software
- ✓ Any unauthorized access through social engineering tools

It is also necessary to contact the cybersecurity department whenever it is necessary to change the configuration of your PC.

Educate and inquire: As a company has a responsibility to educate its employees on cybersecurity, employees need to be willing to learn and not be afraid to ask when they don't know something. As mentioned, it is essential to remain in constant contact with the IT department of the company, which should be contacted both in case of doubts concerning the company policy regarding access of personal devices to company data (BYOD - Bring Your Own Device) and in knowing the necessary processes to back up data in the cloud: even in this case, companies often provide for specific regulations which, if not respected, can lead to the dismissal of the employee. In addition to this, employees should be able to develop technological and digital skills themselves in order to facilitate the support process by the IT department.

As is evident from a reading of these best practices, you don't need to be an IT expert to keep your electronic devices and those of the company you work for safe. Each individual is required to deal - albeit at a micro level - with computer security: that this is the exclusive competence of professionals is now an outdated concept as that of information, in addition to a right, it is now a duty. Cybersecurity awareness is therefore fundamental in an increasingly digitized world, in which technology marks the times and methods of work: from this point of view, understanding how to move in a similar reality - and therefore knowing how to protect yourself from the traps and pitfalls of being connected to a network - is of primary importance today. The commitment of companies, in this sense, is essential: carrying out training courses aimed at implementing the skills of employees in the cybersecurity field is an effective way to train knowledgeable, capable and therefore more productive employees.

CYBERSECURITY AND CYBERWAR IN 2021

THE UNITED STATES IS UNDER CYBER ATTACK

For this reason, a new task force of experts, located within the US Department of Justice - under the responsibility of the FBI - will investigate how to improve the fight against cybercrime, making observations and offering suggestions to the political top.

Development of Cyber Crime Task Force

US Attorney General Jeff Sessions announced the establishment of the new working group in the past few hours, stressing how seriously the DoJ takes threats from cyber space.

Although the scope of the team is extremely broad, the Attorney General told the task force to focus on some issues considered urgent and crucial as a priority. Among these are: the study of efforts to interfere with the US elections (the Russia gate continues to hold the ground); those which could attack and threaten critical infrastructures; the use of the Internet to spread violent ideologies and recruit followers; mass theft of corporate, government and private information; the use of technology to avoid the application of the law; and the mass exploitation of computers and other digital devices to attack US citizens and businesses.

CYBERSECURITY AND CYBERWAR
IN 2021

THE ALARMS

US Attorney Sessions' move comes a few days after the warnings about cyber activism from Russia, China, Iran and North Korea (which over the next year will represent, according to US intelligence, the greatest cyber threat to the country's security) and the dissemination of the numbers released by a very recent report by the Council of Economic Advisers (CEA) of the White House (according to which the malicious computer activities conducted against the United States would have cost in 2016 a sum between 57 and 109 billion dollars).

These actions, targeting private and public entities, have manifested themselves as denial of service attacks, destruction of data and property, business interruption (sometimes for the purpose of collecting ransoms) and theft of proprietary data, intellectual property and financial and strategic information sensitive.

Without forgetting the danger and damage that would ensue (including economically) from a potential cyber-attack against critical infrastructures.

It is therefore urgent for US Attorney Sessions to remedy this by putting in place all available resources.

THE TASK FORCE

To operate, the task force will be chaired by a senior Department official appointed by the Deputy Attorney

General and will consist of representatives from the Department's criminal division, the National Security Division, the United States Attorney's Office community, the Office of Legal Policy, 'Office of Privacy and Civil Liberties, Office of the Chief Information Officer, the ATF, the FBI, the DEA and the US Marshals Service. The Deputy Attorney General may invite representatives of other components of the Department of Justice and other federal agencies to participate in the group, within which he can also create specific subcommittees. The task force will have to deliver a first and detailed report to the Attorney General by the end of June.

CYBERCRIME IS MORE OF A CONCERN TO AMERICANS THAN DRUGS AND MONEY LAUNDERING

44% of respondents say that security problems push them to provide less personal information on websites. 20% are inclined to reduce their online purchases or limit the use of home banking.

70% of Americans surveyed are concerned about the misuse of personal data provided to websites when banking or shopping online, and the vast majority now see cybercrime as a threat to their country. These are some of the key findings from ESET's Cyber Security Barometer, a survey involving 3,500 adults in North America, 2,500 in the United States and 1,000 in Canada.

The result is growing public concern about cybercrime, considering that as many as 9 out of 10 respondents agreed that cybercrime is a major challenge for the entire security of the United States.

The survey even shows that cybercrime is considered a more important threat than drug trafficking or money laundering. What is also worrying is the critical consideration to what has been done so far by the police, whose efforts to combat cybercrime have been judged not sufficient.

AMERICANS AND WEB SECURITY

The most surprising result of the survey was the deep concern respondents expressed about the threats posed by cybercrime and their lack of confidence that the situation will improve anytime soon. About 87% of those involved said they expected an increased risk of becoming a victim of cybercrime.

Other findings of interest are the ways in which Americans are reacting to cybercrime, including a troubling percentage of respondents willing to cut back on their online purchases (19%) or use home banking services due to growing security and privacy concerns (20%). Forty-four percent of respondents said security and privacy concerns led them to provide less personal information on websites.

The report also documents the relationship between concerns related to cybercrime and the actual occurrence of that crime. For example, around 70% of adult Americans surveyed by ESET reported receiving fraudulent emails or phone calls asking for their personal details. A similar percentage expressed concern about this activity. However, while a very large number of people fear that they may be victims of identity theft (86%), the percentage of respondents who reported that they have actually experienced such theft is far less than half (30%).

ESET'S CYBERSECURITY BAROMETER

The results of this survey are the strongest indication that the incidence of systems and data breaches will continue to rise, further undermining trust in technology, unless cyber security and the fight against cybercrime are considered to be among the highest. priority from government agencies and multinationals. Maintaining and increasing that trust is vital to economic well-being, now and in the future.

A new report from USA reveals that Cybercrime cost the global economy almost $600 billion. The software company McAfee, Santa Clara (USA) in collaboration with the Center for Strategic and International Studies (CSIS), today published the "Economic Impact of Cybercrime - No Slowing Down" study, a global report focusing on the significant impact cybercrime has on economies across the country and the world. The report concludes that cybercrime costs businesses nearly $ 600 billion, or 0.8% of global GDP, up from the previous study that estimated global losses at around $ 445 billion in 2014.

The report attributes this growth over three years to the ability of cybercriminals to rapidly adopt new technologies and the relative ease of joining the ranks of cybercrime - including more and more cybercrime centers - and the growing financial sophistication of high-level cybercriminals.

"Digital has transformed nearly every aspect of our lives, including risk and crime, which by digitizing has become more efficient, less risky, more profitable and easier to accomplish than ever before," said Steve Grobman, Chief Technology Officer of McAfee. "Think about the use of ransomware and the attacks in which criminals can outsource much of the work to skilled workers. Cloud-based ransomware-as-a-service providers, efficiently propagate attacks to millions of systems, and attacks are automated to allow minimal human involvement. Adding to these digital currencies that facilitate rapid monetization while minimizing the risk of arrest, we come to the sad conclusion that the $ 600 billion in the pockets of informed criminals is one of the consequences of how our technological advances have transformed the world into a criminal economy, in the same way they have transformed the economy in general".

Banks remain a favorite target of cybercriminals, and nation states are the most dangerous source of cybercrime, as the report notes. Russia, North Korea and Iran are the most active in violating financial institutions, while China is the most active in cyber espionage.

"Our research has shown that Russia is a leader in cybercrime, due to the skill of its hacking community and its contempt for Western law enforcement," added James Lewis, senior vice president of CSIS. "North Korea is in second place, as the nation uses virtual currency theft to fund its regime, and we now see a growing number of cybercrime centers, which are springing up not only in North Korea but also in Brazil, India and Vietnam. "

The report looks at cybercrime in North America, Europe and Central Asia, East Asia and the Pacific, South Asia, Latin America and the Caribbean, Sub-Saharan Africa, the Middle East and North Africa. Unsurprisingly, cybercrime losses are greater in richer countries. However, the countries with the greatest losses (as a percentage of national income) are mid-range countries that are digitized but not yet fully capable of ensuring cybersecurity.

The study did not attempt to measure the cost of all malicious Internet activity, instead focusing on those criminals who illegally gained access to the victim's computer or network. Cybercrime elements identified by the authors include:

- Loss of IP and confidential commercial information

- Online fraud and financial crime, often as a result of stolen personal identification data

- Direct financial manipulation towards listed companies

- Related costs, including costs of interruption of production or services and loss of trust in online activities

- Costs for securing networks, purchasing insurance against cybercrime and costs for recovery in the event of cyber attacks

- Risk of damage to reputation and risk of liability for the company concerned and its brand

To complete the picture on the costs of cyber-attacks, the authors looked at other types of crime for which estimates exist, including maritime piracy, theft and cross-border crime. They note that cybercrime data remains scarce due to an omission of reporting and laxity in most governments around the world in collecting cybercrime data.

We are all aware of the fact that cybercrime represents a growing sector, it is not a purely IT problem, but above all a business risk problem. For this, companies must put the appropriate protection on their data and devices. And don't consider cybersecurity as a problem limited to IT, today IT risk is business risk.

CYBERSECURITY AND CYBERWAR IN 2021

DETRIMENTAL DATA BREACHES

Cyber Risk and Data Breach: causes, consequences and solution.

In an increasingly connected world, Cyber Risk cannot be underestimated.

What is Cyber Risk?

What does it consist of and what damage can it cause?

How can you protect yourself?

In this book, I will answer these questions, describing both the context in which the problem arises and the solution.

Technology has changed our lives in a radical way and has also had a driving effect on economic activities, which today are expressed in a digital dimension.

Along with the opportunities, however, the risks have also evolved exponentially.

How often do you hear about "cyber-attacks"?

CYBERSECURITY AND CYBERWAR
IN 2021

The Hackers have shown that they can overcome any defense and can hit any target, even the most structured of organizations.

In March, a ransomware attack blocked the terminals of the city of Atlanta, forcing more than 8,000 employees to work with pen and paper.

In April, a cyber-attack canceled the video of "Despacito", the musical hit of last summer, from YouTube for a few hours.

Some time ago the website of Symantec, a leading antivirus company and mother of Norton software, was even hit.

It doesn't happen to me anyway ...

This is how risk is often approached, even when it affects us so personally.

The numbers and statistics, however, describe a worrying reality.

CYBER RISK IS A VERY FAST-GROWING PHENOMENON

Over the past year, more than 50% of SMEs have suffered a cyber-attack, for an average cost of about $ 35,000.

CYBERSECURITY AND CYBERWAR IN 2021

There has been a huge growth compared to past years, both due to the effectiveness of the attacks and the economic losses caused.

> Cyber Risk is not the risk of the future, but of the present.

The latest Clusit ICT (Information & Communication Technologies) safety report estimates that in 2017 there were a total of over $10 billion in damages.

It is paradoxical to note that this is a figure ten times higher than what companies invest in their IT security.

WHAT ORIGINS CAN A COMPUTER ATTACK HAVE?

Hacker attacks are carried out by malicious people who, with great skill, infiltrate our systems with very specific objectives.

Equipping ourselves with firewalls and antivirus is a necessary and just precaution, but they do not guarantee the security of the computer system; we must accept that perfect protection does not exist.

Hackers find unwitting accomplices within Organizations: collaborators and employees who, with careless behavior, can favor the entry of dangerous threats.

CYBERSECURITY AND CYBERWAR IN 2021

A USB stick brought from home to download a file, a click on a popup that appears suddenly, or an email opened lightly and that's it.

WHAT DAMAGES CAN CYBER RISK DETERMINE?

This question finds a different answer depending on the reality in which it is asked, depending on the object of the activity, the volume of business and the type of Personal Data managed.

Let's see a Company or a Professional and try to imagine them, also analyzing the direct and indirect economic consequences that can derive from cyber-attacks.

1) THE COST OF CRISIS MANAGEMENT AND RESTORATION

Upon the occurrence of an "accident", or a breach of the information security of our systems, even before worrying about the subsequent indirect consequences, we find ourselves in an urgent need to fix the situation.

When a scan with the antivirus is not enough, the intervention of a team of technicians and IT experts is necessary. However, the incident can also lead to a breach of Personal Data (data breach), or an unauthorized access, their disclosure, or alteration of the information or even their complete erasure.

2) DAMAGES FOR INACTIVITY AND FOR THE LOSS OF DATA

In the time necessary to restore the IT systems from the intrusion, the Company cannot carry out its business regularly.

During the period of total or partial blockage, the Company cannot normally produce income. However, at the same time fixed costs continue to exist and employees' salaries still have to be paid.

The computer systems are reactivated or at least replaced (always bearing the cost), so everything returns to work normally. However, the data breach can also leave another legacy:

Are we sure we can recover the data?

Depending on the scale of the attack, it can, in fact cause their definitive loss, or partial or total damage. Regardless of the outcome, even the recovery attempt already translates into another cost to bear.

3) CLAIMS

Loss or damage has a quantifiable cost, but what about claims that may arise from unauthorized disclosure of Personal Data?

One of the objectives of a hacker attack is precisely the theft of data, also for the purpose of blackmail or extortion against the Data Controller.

Think of the medical records of patients in a Healthcare Facility, the patrimonial and financial data kept by a bank or an accountant, or even the confidential information hidden in the files of a lawyer.

Have you ever heard of Ashley Madison, the famous American extramarital dating site? In 2015, a hacker stole and published the data of over 30 million subscribers.

No example could be clearer and I let you imagine what happened next ...

4) THE LOSS OF REPUTATION

There is no better way to explain how harmful it is for a Company or Professional's business to be with a disgruntled Customer who speaks ill of us in our area or in our target market.

Word gets around very quickly, especially when the news is bad. It can trigger a real flight of customers, with obvious and heavy repercussions on turnover.

To limit the damage, we can initiate communication initiatives aimed at individual customers or the general public, but this means paying for the service of a Call Center or facing the costs of a press release.

So, what to do?

UNDERSTANDING AND PREVENTING RISK

To stem the risk of suffering a breach of the data it holds, every company today has the burden of better understanding the phenomenon of Cyber Risk.

In particular, it is necessary to understand, specifically within each Organization and the Personal Data held and processed therein, what are the vulnerability elements in the face of a hacker attack.

Secondly, always in the interest of protecting its assets, it must put into practice adequate digital, physical and organizational prevention measures.

THE TRANSFER OF RISK AND THE CYBER RISK POLICY

By adopting the new indications and adopting adequate procedures and suitable precautions, a company is safer against Cyber Risk than another that does not do the same.

However, the risk cannot be completely eliminated, no matter how many precautions and prevention measures we can think of adopting.

The risk remains.

There is always a margin of vulnerability to this modern threat and all the economic consequences we have just seen.

Fortunately, there is a solution, at least to eliminate the latter:

We can transfer it.

That's exactly why insurance exists, isn't it?

Along with the new risks of modern society, insurance solutions are also evolving.

Like all events that threaten the assets of a Company or a Professional, Cyber Risk can also be managed with a Policy.

All events attributable to "digital" threats can be considered in the same guarantee.

The direct costs of managing and resolving the crisis can be indemnified, as well as indirect damages due to the interruption of the activity and the financial losses linked to the damage and destruction of the Data.

At the same time, claims for compensation from interested parties can be considered and the cost of reputational defense and crisis mitigation activities can also be used as a guarantee.

You can think of protecting yourself from events such as digital extortion using Ransomware or other cyber fraud.

The protection of the assets of a company and a professional is anything but trivial, especially when threatening it is such a particular risk to be understood and managed like Cyber Risk.

I recommend to approach it with the utmost attention and above all, to do it with the support of someone who proves to be competent and experienced in this new and complex matter.

Cyber Risk is not appreciated in the same way by all companies.

Each proposes its own dedicated solution, but often places significant limits on the guarantee by excluding one or more of the aspects just mentioned.

Never, as in this discourse is it truer that different policies are not all the same.

SMALL CYBERCRIME EVENTS

Cyber security, the 10 most serious violations

2018 was a terrible year for cyber security and in 2019 companies and individuals will have to run for cover: in the last seven years cyber-attacks in the world have registered an exponential growth (+ 240% in 2017 compared to 2011) and in 2018 the trend does not seem to be slowing down.

The digitalization of companies and administrations is rapidly taking place, but investments for the strengthening of public and private IT infrastructures continue to be scarce. Cyber Crime, on the other hand, is a phenomenon that should be fought with funds and tools, since it does not only concern the private life of citizens, but increasingly also the financial and geopolitical plan as evidenced by the recent attack on the German parliament.

Profile information that is stolen by hackers has already been used in the past to carry out targeted cyber-attacks, aimed at individual users, exposing their interests, past experiences, family connections. Having an in-depth understanding of your goals allows cybercriminals to have a

7x greater chance of success than standard attacks. Data breaches represent the phenomenon only in a minimal part:

This is a 'Top 11' based on the official 'data breaches' confirmed by companies. The total number of hacked accounts would be enormously higher if we also included all cyber-attacks denied by companies or suspected and discovered by the media.

THE RANKING OF THE MAJOR IT INTRUSIONS:

1- Marriott: Data of 500 million Starwood Hotels & Resorts guests stolen

The personal data of more than 500 million guests at Marriott International, the largest hotel chain in the world, was exposed to hackers who illegally accessed the Starwood Hotels & Resorts reservation database between 2014 and September 2018. The theft involved guest information numbers, such as addresses, telephone numbers, passport numbers, payment card numbers and expiration dates. The data breach was reported in November 2018.

2 - MyFitnessPal: 150 million hacked users

At the end of February 2018, MyFitnessPal, the eating habits app owned by the Under-Armor company, was hacked resulting in the theft of data from 150 million users, related to usernames, email addresses and passwords. However, the company reported that no payment card data was stolen and is collected separately.

3- Quora: 100 million profiles violated in November

At the end of November Quora, the social network dedicated to information where users can post questions and answers on any topic, discovered that, through an unauthorized third-party application, the profiles of 100 million users would have been compromised. The data involved include names, email addresses, encrypted passwords, user questions and answers.

4- MyHeritage: 92 million family trees violated

On June 4, 2018, the MyHeritage platform, which allows the reconstruction of family trees, announced that it had discovered online a database containing the email addresses and encrypted passwords of 92 million of its users. According to the company, however, no further sensitive data in the system would have been violated or disclosed.

5- Cambridge Analytica: the media case of 2018

One of the most striking cases of all 2018 is certainly that of Cambridge Analytica: in 2015 an app, ' This is Your Digital life', promised to predict the personality of users while improperly transmitting information to third parties, including Cambridge Analytica, the data analytics company also hired by President Trump to create targeted election announcements. Only 270,000 Facebook users actually installed the offending app, but by leveraging the Facebook Friendship Network data sharing rules of 2015, the app was able to gather information on 87 million users.

6- Google+: 52.5 million violations before the social network was closed

Google+, the social network of the Mountain View giant, had to face two dangerous vulnerabilities in 2018. The first in March that affected 500,000 profiles, the second, much more serious, in December with the data breach of 52.5 million of users. This last data breach prompted the platform managers to accelerate its closure in April 2019.

7- Facebook: 50 million affected in the Zuckerberg social network

On September 25, 2018, Facebook engineers discovered a serious flaw affecting 50 million profiles. Attackers exploited a vulnerability in Facebook's code that affected 'View As' mode, a feature that allows people to see what their profile looks like to someone else.

8- Chegg: 40 million compromised profiles

CYBERSECURITY AND CYBERWAR IN 2021

On September 19, 2018, Chegg, an American company specializing in educational services and textbook rental, discovered that in the previous months an unauthorized application had gained access to a corporate database that housed chegg.com user data. Due to this vulnerability, the usernames, e-mail addresses, shipping addresses and encrypted passwords of 40 million active registered users were compromised.

9- Ticketfly: 27 million concert fans with a compromised profile

The famous ticket buying platform for events and concerts, Ticketfly was hit in late May by a serious cyber-attack that compromised various personal information including the names, addresses, emails and telephone numbers of 27 million users. According to the platform operators, however, financial information such as credit card numbers would not have been stolen.

10- Sacramento Bee: 19.5 million profiles hacked

In February, a hacker seized two databases run by The Sacramento Bee, a Sacramento, California newspaper. One of the archives contained California voter registration data provided by the Secretary of State for journalistic purposes, while the other database contained archived contact information for subscribers to the newspaper. Following the theft, the cybercriminals demanded a ransom in exchange for accessing the seized data. The newspaper rejected and deleted the databases to prevent further attacks from exploiting them in the future. The two databases contained 19.4 million users and 53,000 users respectively.

11 - Orange Park: Cybercriminals stole $ 491,000 from an American town.

Cybercriminals stole $ 491,000 from an American city in Florida (Orange Park) using infected emails sent to multiple city hall officials. The infection started when a city hall official opened the first infected email. Similar messages were then sent to other officials, and some of them even opened the attachment. Opening the attachment introduced a virus into the city's computer system that allowed the hacker to tap into information related to the city's Wells Fargo bank account.

The malware sent the login data for online banking. With this data, the cybercriminals gained access to the online bank account and transferred $ 491,000 to an account with Deutsche Bank. The cyber criminals have not been arrested or identified. Following the event, the city implemented new security measures covering its computer system.

CYBERSECURITY AND CYBERWAR IN 2021

How Not To Get Easily HACKED?

How to tell if you have been hacked and what to do

From Facebook to Google, passing through Netflix. Sometimes our accounts get compromised, here's what to do when it happens.

We are all, in one way or another, potentially vulnerable to the threat of cybercriminals - or criminal hackers - having access to our information. The average person is likely to face fewer sophisticated threats than, say, a politician, activist, or CEO of a Fortune 500 company. Higher-profile figures can be targeted with spear phishing emails.

There is value in everything you do online - from Facebook and Netflix to online banking and shopping. If one of our accounts is compromised, stolen credentials or our bank details can be used online. While Facebook, Twitter, Instagram and other social networks are less likely to hold our credit card information, there are other types of risk.

But finding out if you've been hacked can be a rather complicated task.

We may wait for proof by losing control of our accounts, although like everything, it's best to be proactive and prevent this from happening in the future.

LEARN TO RECOGNIZE SUSPICIOUS BEHAVIOR

The most obvious sign, of course, is when we are able to detect substantial and concrete changes. We may not be able to log into our Google account or there may have been a suspicious purchase charged to one of our bank accounts. However, before one of our accounts is compromised, there may be other warning signs. The account someone is trying to log into may warn you of unusual login attempts - for example, Facebook and Google will send you notifications and emails alerting you to attempts to log into your account. This usually happens if someone has attempted to enter and failed, but alerts can also be when someone has successfully logged in from unknown locations. Not a day goes by without some company, app or website experiencing a data breach - from Adobe to Foodora. These data leaks can include phone numbers, passwords, credit card details and other personal information that would allow criminals to compromise our online identity. Obviously, the burden of notification of this breach should always be borne by the company that was attacked, but if you want to be proactive, there are many third-party notification services that can warn you of the possible compromise of your data.

Take back control

Once we have confirmation that our account has been hacked, the "hard" part begins. Regaining control of an account can be challenging - depending on who has access to it - and there is a good chance that this will involve a considerable amount of "paperwork": from telling everyone you know that your email is been compromised to notifying law enforcement. First of all, we need to get in touch with the company that manages our account. Each company will have their own policies, procedures and recovery steps when dealing with compromised accounts - these can easily be found through an online search. When recovering a hacked online account, you are likely to go through several stages depending on whether or not you can still access it.

If you can log into your account, companies will often ask you how it was compromised and provide you with suggestions on steps to take.

If you can't log in, you will likely be asked to provide more information on how the account was used (previous passwords, email addresses, security questions, and more). Recovering your account through the pre-set procedures of the company where you were hacked is the first step to regain control.

The other actions you take are specific to what has been breached.

For example, if you manage to re-enter a previously hacked email account, it's worth checking your settings to make sure they haven't been manipulated. You may have enabled the setting for automatically forwarding all your emails to another account. Another universal and fundamental step is to change the password of the attacked account and of all the others that use the same password.

Get safe

The best way to reduce the chances of being hacked is to limit the attack surface. It goes without saying that more attention we pay to our online behaviors means less chance of being attacked. Personal information is the key to a successful attack, so minimizing our private data available online should push the attacker to the next less fortunate victim. When thinking about your online presence, you should take into account how much information is proactively spreading.

In addition to a password manager, multifactor authentication (MFA or multi- factor authentication) should be turned on for as many sites and services that offer it as possible. Most commonly this is an SMS message, an authentication application, or a physical security key.

CYBERSECURITY AND CYBERWAR IN 2021

Protecting yourself from hackers is not complicated: just don't make these mistakes that are still all too common.

Out there, on the Net, there is no shortage of malicious people hunting for information: simple addresses, credit card numbers, banking information and so on are precious goods, and there is always someone who eventually falls foul of this crime network.

The fault may lie with a still unknown and therefore incorrect vulnerability, a security software that does not do its duty or the overwhelming ability of the hacker on duty, but more often those who fall into a trap find themselves in that situation because they have made a mistake.

In fact, there are some behaviors that must absolutely be avoided if you want to increase your safety margin: below, we present eight things not to do if you want to stay out of trouble.

1. Choose obvious passwords

It is the most repeated advice and also the most disregarded. While everyone knows that the password doesn't have to be trivial, in the end many choose combinations that are not only obvious, but downright embarrassing so easily they can be guessed.

The ranking of the most commonly stolen passwords, published every year by SplashData, is here to prove it: in it there are always things like abc123, qwerty,

111111 and, on top, the immortal 123456, not to mention passwords.

2. Always use the same password

To many, once they have built a nice password, full of all the elements we have recommended and containing enough characters, it seems a waste to use it only once. And it becomes one password less to remember.

The five attack techniques most exploited by hackers

1. Breach of weak passwords: 80% of cyberattacks rely on targeting weak, non-compliant passwords to choose a strong password.

2. Malware attacks: a catchy link, an infected USB key, an application (even for smartphones) that is not what it appears to be: these are all systems that can install malware on PCs.

3. Phishing emails: they look like messages from official or personal sources but the links they contain lead to infected sites.

4. Social engineering is responsible for 29% of security breaches, with losses per attack ranging from $ 25,000 to $ 100,000 and data stealing.

5. Ransomware: those programs that "hold hostage" the user's data or a website until the user pays a sum to unlock it.

On the other hand, remembering many passwords that are always different can actually be difficult: in these cases, you can rely on password managers (one very famous, but not the only one, is LastPass) who take care of remembering them for us, and they protect the safe in which they keep them with a Master Password. Obviously, this will be protected as if it is what is most sacred to us in the world.

3. Open the attachments

We could have written that the mistake not to make is "open attachments from strangers" but in reality, the simple indication of the sender can be misleading: malware creators have long since learned to exploit the address books of infected computers to pass themselves off as friends and thus reach new victims.

Malware spreaders have learned that attachments are often opened without much thought, "just for a look" and perhaps with some confidence because the extension indicates that it is a harmless file.

Despite the progress made by security systems, it still happens that what appeared to be a harmless PDF was actually an executable file capable of infecting the PC by avoiding the antivirus. Open with care and hope that it's not too late.

4. Click on the links received by email

This error is a close relative of the previous one, and is the reason why phishing campaigns have not yet died out: they simply work.

The typical deception is that consisting of an email that seems to come from a reliable sender (the bank, the post office, the credit card issuing institution ...) and which, in official language, requires you to click on a link kindly provided in the body of the email itself to "update your data".

To avoid falling into the trap, just check the link before clicking; sometimes the links are masked (if the message is in HTML) and appear to point to a legitimate domain, but a look at the source of the email always reveals the deception.

5. Shopping at suspicious online auctions

eBay, and similar sites, are a great convenience and often host many genuine offers. Unfortunately, though, even here the bad guys are lurking.

A deal that looks too good is already a bit suspicious, but there is another way to make sure that the seller is good: feedback.

Always taking a look at the opinions left by those who have already traded with the seller we are interested in is a quick and easy way to understand if we are facing an honest person or a scam artist.

6. Enter sensitive data on unsafe sites

The habit of shopping online, with systems that all in all resemble each other from one site to another, has created in users a sort of "autopilot" that carries out the sale without paying attention to too much detail.

Unfortunately, that's what those on the hunt for personal information count on.

Still too many sites, due to the laziness of those who manage them or for whatever other reason, allow users to enter their personal data (including credit card number) without using an encrypted connection.

Realizing this is simple: if there is a padlock on the far left of the browser's address bar, perhaps accompanied by the letters "**https**" (some browsers hide it, simply showing the padlock), then the connection is secure and the data is encrypted before be transmitted. Even if they were intercepted, they would be unusable.

7. Use open Wi-Fi networks

Certainly, public Wi-Fi networks, which can be accessed without even having to enter a password, are a great convenience and, when you are out and about, they allow you to save on the consumption of mobile data traffic.

However, many routers also used in hotels to provide free Wi-Fi are affected by a serious vulnerability, which allows those who exploit it to intercept other people's web traffic.

History also shows that open Wi-Fi networks are very popular with hackers who want to launch DDoS attacks and, in general, it is best not to use them if you intend to use sites where personal data is required.

8. Do not use two-step authentication

Many online service providers, from Google down, offer the possibility of two-step authentication: in addition to the password, they also require you to enter a code that they send to the user's mobile phone.

In this way, anyone who had taken possession of the password would still be locked out of the service they are trying to access illegally.

Many users find it an interesting protection, but annoying, because the mobile phone has to be at hand, it has to be charged, it has to be in range of a signal ... So, they don't use it, and they put themselves in danger.

5 MORE TRICKS TO AVOID BEING HACKED

From the dangers of cloud computing to the use of VPNs, some important tips to make life difficult for the bad guys. Although the so-called "hackers" can count on good technical skills, all too often the habits of users facilitate their work.

We have already provided a first set of tips. In the next few pages, we present some other tricks to follow to avoid delivering themselves into the hands of malicious people who are waiting for nothing but a false move by their victims.

1. Avoid cloud computing

It may seem strange, given that cloud solutions are being proposed with increasing insistence, but just think of glaring events such as the theft of private images of celebrities - the scandal known as The Fappening - to understand how things really are.

Handing over your private data to a reality over which you have no control means losing control over that data as well: there is no network that does not risk being violated and, in that case, it is the users who pay the price.

It is therefore good to avoid exposing sensitive information by saving it in the cloud and under the illusion that it will be safe there forever: if possible, avoid cloud computing.

2. Beware of security questions

Many services allow you to choose a "security question" that will be presented if the password is lost: the idea is that only the legitimate account holder knows the answer and, therefore, whoever knows it is the legitimate owner of the account. 'account.

Unfortunately, as social networks advance, certain personal information typically used to draft security questions can be recovered with some ease.

Therefore, it is better not to use real data when indicating the answer to the security question: a little memory effort will help protect yourself.

3. Secure your home Wi-Fi network

Popular Wi-Fi routers aren't set up to offer maximum security from the factory.

Often the wireless network they create is open, or offers old WEP encryption. Also, the admin password is always set to a default value (sometimes admin, sometimes 1234 or something just as simple) which is the same for all routers of the same model, or even the same manufacturer.

Before using your shiny new router, it is essential to open the configuration page and tighten the security links.

4. Avoid linking accounts

Linking different accounts is a practical way to easily manage the digital flow of information, but it does expose you to an obvious risk: if one account is hacked, the consequences will be felt on others as well.

For example, if the personal and corporate Twitter accounts are linked, the theft of the password of the former will make life easier for those who want to violate the latter as well.

5. Use a VPN

Those who are particularly sensitive to their privacy often make use of a VPN, because the traffic crossing this network is protected with an end-to-end encryption, and is thus protected from intrusions.

Their use is particularly recommended if you are using a public Wi-Fi network, perhaps because you are in a hotel or are using an airport hotspot.

There are several companies that offer free VPN services, which once accessed promote their most complete package, which is generally a subscription one; an example of one of these widely used, is Hotspot Shield.

CYBERSECURITY IN THE 2000'S V 2020.

2010-2020: a decade of cyber "insecurity"

In this period, the "incidents" of digital security increased. It's a side effect of digitalization and a lack of corporate attention.

Not all alarms and security breaches are created equal. And in the decade that began in 2010 some are little more than headlines, while others have been truly serious incidents that have forever changed the way experts deal with these kinds of problems, especially in the corporate world.

In fact, on the media and on social networks we talk every day about this or that malware, this or that incident, this or that data loss. But some cases are really important, while others are little more than marketing for antivirus manufacturers.

One of the deep reasons for this increase in cyber-insecurity is to be traced back to digitization. The evolution and growing pervasiveness of these change frameworks have in fact increased radically while society as a whole - from legislators to users - has not developed an adequate awareness and culture of cybersecurity at the same speed.

If you look at the historical statistics of the security vendors, it turns out that in the last ten years we have passed into the trillions of security incidents and vulnerabilities. Importantly we can point out six that instead had such an impact that they forever changed the history of technology and our relationship with it.

2010: IRANIAN NUCLEAR INFRASTRUCTURE

The attack is "signed" by the US and Israel, according to experts. For sure Stuxnet, the digital weapon, was not a malware like the others. Stuxnet was introduced inside Iranian nuclear plants by modifying the operating cycle of centrifuges for the separation of uranium, bringing them to saturation and breaking. It is the first time that a digital attack has been thought of as a real sabotage tool in the physical world with a cyberwar scenario. The Iranians then took Stuxnet's code and reused it to attack targets like Saudi Arabia. It is currently available on the Dark Web.

2013: Target

The Target store chain in 2013 said it suffered an attack that led to the theft of credit card data and various other personal details (names, addresses, phone numbers, emails) of 110 million people. There have been hundreds of similar attacks over the decade, but this was the most notorious and led to the loss of 46% year-over-year quarterly revenue due to news of the breach. Experts learned a lot from the ways of the attack, which exploited the weakness of a third-party vendor providing outsourced services. After the CEOs, CIOs and other managers resigned, the boards and executives of other companies began to pay attention to the problem.

2014: Sony

In November 2014, North Korea stole a series of Sony Motion Pictures emails as revenge for a film that parodied the North Korean leader. Released on the Dark Web, the emails also included private and embarrassing exchanges about the company's actors and actresses, which led to the resignation of Sony's all-powerful head of studios, Amy Pascal. An additional incentive to defend companies not only from the loss of customer data, direct physical or digital damage, but also to cover the reputational damage that the leak entails. A risk that has repositioned the priority of cybersecurity on the agenda of top managers, and has also made North Korea emerge as a cybersuperpower.

2017: NotPetya

NotPetya ransomware, the digital child of WannaCry but much more powerful and deleterious, has blocked thousands of companies around the world. Merck has had to stop its vaccine production, Maersk has stopped shipments of its container ships, Cadbury has stopped producing milk and cheese, while FedEx and Reckitt Benckiser have had to stop deliveries. The effect of the ransomware has been enormous and profound, with ramified consequences, starting with the class actions brought against large companies by angry consumers, and the payment of millionaire compensation to users. It is the birth of the cyber-insurance market, which become the protagonists of the next two years as the only resource to protect citizens' data from the risks of ransomware to which cities are also exposed, especially in the USA. Warren Buffet decides not to invest in this sector because, "while we can statistically predict hurricane or earthquake risk, cyber risk is totally unpredictable and in the long term not convenient for an insurer".

2017: Equifax

Criminals, exploiting a seemingly minor vulnerability in open source software, find a way to break into the systems of Equifax, a private provider of financial services for the management of US taxpayers' data, and steal the database containing Social Security numbers and other details for the credit score of halves of Americans in addition to those of Canadians and Britons. Perhaps not the largest data theft in history, certainly the most toxic to public administrations. The CEO Richard Smith resigned two weeks later while the IOC is accused of having used information about the security breach to sell company stock before publication. Equifax continued to pay hundreds of millions of dollars in damages to American citizens.

2018: Marriott

The large hotel chain suffers the theft of its guest data in mid-2018: half a billion people affected, with just 5 million passport numbers stolen. Apparently, a cyber theft like many others, with relatively few direct consequences. In reality, this cyberattack had devastating medium-term consequences for the company: the data theft came following the acquisition of Starwood Resorts (bought in 2016 for $ 13.3 billion) that had probably been losing data for years. Except that at the time of the acquisition, Marriott saw neither the vulnerabilities nor the attack. In short, it was a due diligence problem during the acquisition, which subsequently led to numerous lawsuits filed by the shareholders with a growth that practically brought the hotel chain to its knees. This was a rude awakening for many corporate executives about to make an acquisition or merger.

THE IMPACT OF CYBERSECURITY ON THE ECONOMY AND DEMOCRACY OF THE COUNTRY: THE ROLE OF SCIENTIFIC RESEARCH

The existence of thousands of networks makes it difficult even to have a snapshot of who is connected to it and the layering of software programs and protocols developed

CYBERSECURITY AND CYBERWAR

IN 2021

over Forty years. leads to a complexity that generates vulnerabilities (software errors, incorrect configurations and weaknesses in protocols) that are exploited by cybercriminals to steal data or cause damage.

Cybersecurity is considered one of the main emergencies in the world, together with climate change and immigration, and concrete initiatives are being studied to address this emergency. Blocking of company operations, surreptitious control of critical infrastructure services, theft of intellectual property or information crucial for the survival of a company, are examples of the threats that a country must also face. The recent campaigns of the so-called WannaCry and notPetya malware were the visible events of an impressive series of attacks in every corner of the planet.

In an increasingly digitalized world, cyber-attacks raise alarm in the population, cause significant damage to the economy and endanger the very safety of citizens when they hit distribution networks of essential services such as health, energy, transport, not to mention the critical infrastructures of modern society. In entire sectors of industry, such as mechanics, shipbuilding, tourism, agri-food and transport, they could suffer heavy downsizing of turnover due to attacks perpetrated in cyberspace by sovereign states or competitors.

A successful cyberattack could be a moment of no return for a company's credibility, business development and the ability to sell products under healthy competition. Equally, a successful cyber-attack could destabilize the stock market by plunging entire countries into chaos, or blocking gas supplies in the winter or managing the municipal waste cycle.

Many times, the damage of cyber-attacks depends on a weak link and often this is the human factor. Man is now an integral part of cyberspace and represents the most important and unpredictable vulnerability of this macrosystem. A wrong click can in some cases destroy any technological defense line of an apparatus, an organization, a country. They are the first to open the doors for criminals to the sites, networks and databases of their organizations, with dangerous and unpredictable effects.

Not only industry, but also democracy can be subject to cyber-attacks. Fake news is the evolution of the social engineering-based attacks: created and spread through cyberspace, false information tends to confuse and destabilize the citizens of a country, by immersing them in an uncontrolled informational space with a collection of almost infinite sources news.

A country that does not put cybersecurity at the center of its digital transformation policies is therefore a country that puts its economic prosperity and independence at serious risk.

in 2016, In the face of a high vulnerability of the corporate system, spending on cyber security was modest: the median company allocated just 4,530 dollars to the prevention of attacks, or 15% of the annual gross salary of an average worker. However, there were important differences between sectors: the figure rose to $ 19,080 among Information and Communication Technology (ICT) firms, to drop to $ 3,420 among low-tech firms. Almost all companies claimed to use at least anti-virus software and two-thirds to train employees in the safe use of computing devices; on the other hand, the habit of encrypting data, adopted by less than a third of non-ICT companies, was not widespread.

As for the damage caused by the attacks, various data show that in most cases the direct monetary impact is limited; However, it must be taken into account that the economic impact of an attack is often not limited to the immediate cost, but involves damage to the image and can allow indirect attacks to be carried out, leveraging the vulnerability of one subject to hit another.

As citizens and businesses, we must therefore be ready to monitor and protect our digital world. The defense and monitoring of our cyberspace must come into our way of life, just as the advent of automobiles made it natural to look left and right before crossing a busy street. Keeping our devices under control, updating their software, knowing our possible vulnerabilities, are actions that must be part of a continuous process of IT risk management.

In this context, scientific research plays an essential role in the development of methodologies and tools to evaluate the security level of our digital world and develop strategies and solutions to increase its security level. During 2017-2018, the scientific community, coordinated by the National Cybersecurity Laboratory of CINI, produced a White

CYBERSECURITY AND CYBERWAR IN 2021

Paper in which the main research challenges in the sector are presented and a series of project activities are proposed to the political decision-make, to provide the national cyberspace a state-of-the-art level of protection for scientific research.

And now, let's see the impact of cyber-attacks on the cornerstones of our society and, therefore, starting from what is produced in the White Paper, we elaborate and present, in a synthetic way, the main scientific challenges for cybersecurity research.

Impact on the backbones of our society

Digital transformation is affecting all sectors of our economy and will profoundly change society, our relationships and the way we do industry. Digital transformation, both at an industrial and a societal level, is characterized by the development of systems that have a dual nature: physical and virtual. The physical system is superimposed on a cyber level (e.g. sensors and actuators, calculation, communication and storage systems) in order to increase its efficiency, reliability, adaptability and security. The Internet of Things, guaranteeing the connection of the objects of the physical world to the Internet, constitutes the connecting technology between the two levels, and information flows continuously between the two levels.

Typical examples are Manufacturing 4.0 (or Industry 4.0) and Smart Cities. In fact, these systems operate on two

CYBERSECURITY AND CYBERWAR
IN 2021

levels: the physical level (the factory, the city) with its infrastructures (the machinery in the case of the factory, the roads, the electricity grid, the means of transport, etc., in the case of city), and a second level, the cyber level, which contains a "virtual" and interactive representation of the physical level, generated and maintained through the pervasive use of ICT technologies. The objective of the cyber level is to continuously monitor the state of the physical infrastructures, adapting them to the needs of production / citizens in order to combine efficiency and quality of products / services. An attack on the cyber level can, therefore, render the physical level (eg the transport system in a city, rather than the machinery or logistics system in a factory) inoperable, or even dangerous.

In this context, cybersecurity is everywhere: in hardware, in software, in interconnection systems, in business processes, in contracts, in policies, in the human factor, in cybersocial interactions. Cybersecurity therefore becomes the essential element of this new dimension to ensure an adequate level of security over time for our relationships, our business, our democracies.

Democracy

For a democratic state it is essential to guarantee high levels of cybersecurity, both to protect national security (including the protection of free elections and electoral campaigns from external interference) and to guarantee the country's economic well-being and growth. In many countries, methods and technologies for electronic voting are being tested; however, these tools must be used with caution, especially for general elections. In fact, there are no 100% secure computer systems and the chances of success of an attack depend on how much an attacker is willing to invest and, therefore, on how much one can potentially earn from the attack. Well, in the case of political elections, there can be many subjects interested in investing a lot, with the aim of governing, controlling or destabilizing a country. To avoid risks, national strategies must be developed that align national security needs with those of economic growth and promote security right from the design of all digital policies.

Finance

The digital transformation was also the occasion for a radical change in the business models of banks and insurance companies. Many banking services are provided via mobile devices and have seen the entry of global operators such as Amazon and Google into the payments area. The expansion of the ecosystem to non-bank operators obviously poses serious problems in terms of operational security. The digitization of insurance services, on the other hand, entails an increasing use of context data associated with transactions or collected by IoT (Internet of Things) devices for the execution of online analytics. This use has increased the unit value of financial data on the illegal market and made them a more attractive target for attackers. The financial sector has in fact suffered, in recent years, unprecedented attacks, characterized by distributed and coordinated attack vectors. The analysis of these attacks allows us to identify three fundamental threats:

- temporary impairment of the functionality of banking and insurance services;
- large-scale organized theft of banking and financial data;
- violation of the integrity of the data present within the banking / insurance system.

Transportation

Guaranteeing cybersecurity in the transport sector requires considering closely related and interdependent areas: vehicles, services and infrastructures. For vehicles and services, the spread of IoT devices, which makes it possible to increase passenger comfort and offer innovative services, introduces challenges both for the processing of the myriad of data generated, and for the immeasurable increase in the attack surface and their capillarity and pervasiveness. In the short term it will become unavoidable for our country to equip itself with infrastructures that in the medium / long term allow the completely autonomous driving of road vehicles and the use of drones in urban areas; to do this it is important to know that a radical paradigm shift is essential.

Beyond the necessary legislative adjustments, it is necessary to provide for the introduction of rules that bind the project and subsequent construction of these new infrastructures to the concept and practice of security by design, as it is neither conceivable nor tolerable that it will be repeated for these infrastructures. It is also necessary to define new standards capable of integrating the wide range of international standards in the world of transport, defined to address problems of safety, quality assurance of service and fault tolerance, with the security problems introduced by new technologies. and, in particular, from the IoT.

Industry

Digital transformation will profoundly change the way of doing industry in the future. The new industry will completely lose the concept of physical perimeter that has characterized it until now, thus finding itself immersed in cyberspace, with suppliers and customers in a single large virtual space. IoT, artificial intelligence, the cloud and enterprise technologies are completely eliminating the perimeter, moving data and services out of it. For this reason, there are numerous risks related to cybersecurity at the company level: however, in too many work contexts, this is still considered exclusively a burden and not an asset.

This process must lead to the launch of personnel training and cyber risk management processes based on internationally recognized best practices. Hence the primary need for the presence of a sustainable certification system that can help a company orient itself on the various products to be acquired, having the guarantee of an adequate level of safety.

COMMUNICATION AND PRESS

Informing and educating about cybersecurity is a challenge that affects everyone: citizens, businesses, institutions and universities. Linguistic confusion leads to the use of words that refer to distorting concepts. A typical example is the word hacker and hacking activities. The mistaken equivalence that identifies hackers with cybercriminals raises irrational fears and deprives us of a theory and practice where hackers can be cybersecurity's best allies.

Being a hacker, a virtuoso of programming, an expert in networks and computers, is the necessary, but not sufficient, condition to illegally penetrate a protected computer system. Hackers acting without criminal targets can be formidable defenders of our cyberspace, and many indeed are.

Scientific research to guarantee cybersecurity

Scientific research is essential to address the challenges that cybercrime poses to the digital society. The challenges concern both scientific research and technological innovation. In many cases, in addition to obtaining theoretical results, it is necessary to create prototype systems aimed at a more rapid industrialization of the solutions. Given the diversity of objectives and skills needed to face these challenges, a strong synergy is needed between the world of scientific research and that of industrial research.

In particular, companies will play a fundamental role - within an integrated system - in the subsequent prototyping and industrialization of the proposed solutions. The relationship between research and industry must be of a circular type, in the sense that the problems faced must be defined in a shared way; innovative approaches defined on the basis of scenarios and requirements identified in a collaborative way; the solutions developed will then be modified and gradually refined on the basis of industrial experiences in the field. All this will allow for a timely and effective technology transfer. Finally, an important role is assigned to the Government and the institutions in terms of defining the necessary regulatory frameworks and implementing funding programs to address the challenges detailed below. The rest of this section is devoted to presenting and discussing three main lines of research, and specifically: Enabling Actions, Enabling Technologies and Producing Technologies to Protect.

Enabling actions

This area includes the actions necessary to make the threat management cycle more secure: from protecting critical applications to creating a national threat bank, from defending against cyber or social attacks to the malicious use of Artificial Intelligence.

Network Services Protection

Networked applications and services are rapidly becoming the preferred channel for users to access digital services provided by companies.

These applications allow you to carry out operations that require high security standards, both for the sensitivity of the data processed and for the economic or reputational impact that an abuse of the service by malicious people would entail. Often advanced services are provided by combining different systems that interact, giving life to real ecosystems.

Since the data present in the ecosystems are generated by interoperable applications of different levels of sophistication, complexity and security, the risks of their subtraction are amplified. In these cases, the safety analysis is particularly complex, as problems can emerge from the interaction between components, even when each of them has been well designed, tested and implemented. It is therefore important to have methodologies, tools and environments to evaluate, analyze and measure the safety level of the individual components, of the systems obtained through their interaction, and of the ecosystems deriving from the composition of other systems.

This results in a number of scientific challenges and research objectives.

Malware detection

Malware represent one of the primary threats in cybersecurity, as they are both vehicles to access a remote system, to control it and to compromise it (botnet), as well as a tool for theft or destruction of information present in computer systems. Breaches caused by malware (malicious code) account for 69% of the breaches surveyed, with an annual increase of 10%. Behind the creation and distribution of new malware lies extensive code reuse. Detailed analysis has highlighted how many codes of this kind are obtained through re-engineering of pre-existing malware, consequently limiting the success of traditional protection systems based on signature detection, as new malware.

Fight against Cybercrime

The last ten years have been characterized by a huge growth in the number of cybersecurity incidents of a very heterogeneous nature: from identity theft to cyber espionage, from financial scams to ransomware. This phenomenon is the consequence of a paradigmatic evolution in the world of cybercrime, which today operates according to a crime as a service model in which extremely powerful and complex hacking tools become accessible at low prices and can be used without requiring in-depth technical skills. At the same time, the complexity of the attacks has also grown.

The attacks have shown how cybercriminals are able to infiltrate complex organizations, take complete control of large-scale systems, and persist in such systems for years, effectively hiding their presence and actions. This type of particularly complex and structured attacks, typically known as Advanced Persistent Threat (APT), today represents a fundamental problem for all large organizations (public and private) operating in a global context. The asymmetry between attackers and defenders continues to grow: the time required to penetrate a system is reduced thanks to increasingly effective attack tools, while the time required to discover and eradicate the presence of a cyber threat grows; reducing this asymmetry is a fundamental objective.

Detection of Fake News

Protecting decision-making processes from disinformation and counter-information activities is a vital activity for every country. Historically this is a task entrusted to the intelligence services and the game has so far been played in a scenario in which the dissemination of information and knowledge took place through newspapers, party organs or academic hierarchies. The Internet has radically changed the way knowledge is created and accessed, upsetting all mediation systems in favor of direct access to a multitude of contents. The complexity of the phenomena of reality is apparently accessible to all, but not always in an understandable way: our cognitive system struggles to adapt to new concepts such as uncertainty, complexity, probability, tending to favor simpler and therefore reassuring syntheses and narratives. In this new context, the ancient problem of the spread of fake news and its consequences must be faced.

The process of spreading false information passes through a series of cognitive mechanisms that lead to the acquisition of information related to one's own vision of the world and to ignore the contrary theses; we all tend to form highly polarized groups on shared narratives. This makes the dissemination of false information fruitful for spurious purposes, both economic and in the service of other interests, which can have a considerable weight in the public debate.

The problem is serious and delicate and science in general, and information technology in particular, must play a decisive and fundamental role in this challenge. Below are the main objectives to be pursued. Before doing so, we believe it useful to underline that to achieve them it is necessary to adopt a multidisciplinary approach, implementing a series of initiatives and synergies on several levels to ensure a better understanding of the problem in the current context and to develop effective responses through synergies between the various actors of the information system.

The technological solution alone is not sufficient due to the complexity of the phenomenon and the analysis can neither be algorithmic only, nor left exclusively to man.

Artificial intelligence

Artificial intelligence (AI) deserves a separate discussion as it must be seen both as a technology to be protected and as a technology to be protected from. Machine learning capabilities are growing at an unprecedented rate. These technologies are the basis of very useful applications, ranging from machine translation to image analysis in medicine, and it is to be expected that there will be many more such applications in the short and long term. AI is therefore attracting a lot of attention; less attention has been paid so far to the fact that AI can be misused. In this section we want to examine the potential security threats arising from malicious uses of AI, seeking to identify ways to predict, prevent and mitigate these threats.

As the capabilities of AI become more powerful and widespread, it will increasingly be used in the context of cybersecurity: the costs of attacks on computer systems can be significantly reduced by the scalable use of AI- based systems : these can be used to carry out quickly, and without great additional costs, activities that would normally require human work, intelligence and competence. And the attacks enabled by the use of AI can be particularly effective, finely targeted, difficult to attribute, and capable of exploiting the vulnerabilities of the AI systems used by defenders. Below we consider three security domains separately, illustrating the possible changes to threats within these domains through representative examples.

Digital security

The use of AI to automate tasks related to the execution of cyber-attacks will reduce the gap between the scope and effectiveness of the attacks. This can expand the threat associated with work-intensive cyber-attacks (such as spear phishing). We also expect new attacks that exploit human vulnerabilities (e.g. through the use of speech synthesis for impersonation), existing software vulnerabilities (e.g. through automated hacking) or AI system vulnerabilities (e.g. through adversarial learning or machine learning in hostile environment and data poisoning).

Physical security

The use of AI to automate tasks related to the execution of attacks with drones and other physical systems (for example, through the use of autonomous weapon systems) can widen the threats associated with such attacks. We also expect new attacks that subvert cybernetic systems (for example, causing autonomous vehicle crashes) or that involve physical systems that would be impossible to direct remotely (for example, a swarm of thousands of micro drones).

Political security

The use of AI to automate surveillance tasks (e.g. mass-collected data analysis), persuasion (e.g. targeted propaganda creation) and deception (e.g. video manipulation) can expand the threats associated with invasion of the privacy and social manipulation. New attacks are also to be expected that exploit an improved ability to analyze human behavior, moods and beliefs based on available data.

Enabling technologies

The programs in this category aim to strengthen some of the basic technologies to be used to protect data, limit attacks and their effects and, in general, to increase the resilience of systems through targeted security by design solutions. In particular, in this section, the hardware architectures that guarantee higher levels of security, cryptography, blockchain, biometric and quantum technologies are considered.

Hardware architectures

Similarly, to what happens for software, data and communication infrastructures, hardware must also be designed, built, tested, used and maintained taking into account possible cyber-attacks and their consequences. The hardware runs the software and is, in fact, the last line of defense: if the hardware is corrupted, all the mechanisms introduced to secure the software (at any level) can be useless. Inadequately protected hardware can be the weak link in the chain, becoming an easy gateway to the system, its functions and the data it holds.

As with software, hardware vulnerabilities can result from design errors or malicious components intentionally inserted into devices. Furthermore, unlike software, hardware can be observed and controlled, and therefore physically attacked, from the outside.

The vulnerabilities deriving from the hardware can only be corrected by modifying the program and are therefore in fact destined to remain present forever inside the devices.

Encryption

Encryption is the basic technique for guaranteeing information that is secure from the point of view of the indecipherability of messages. It is in fact one of the fundamental mechanisms for data protection and identification, used pervasively for example when we connect to our bank via the Web, use ATMs, credit cards and disable the device that immobilizes our car. In recent years, the number of cryptographic systems vulnerabilities has increased considerably. Systems considered inviolable until a few years ago are today considered insecure. Furthermore, the advent of quantum computers will undermine standard encryption systems, such as RSA, and it is therefore of fundamental importance to study post quantum algorithms that are robust.

Biometrics

Verification of digital identity is an essential element for the security of a system, whether IT or not. Traditional methods of recognizing individuals are based on keys, tokens, identity documents and passwords. These approaches, while still valid, are showing all their limits in terms of security and above all, of usability. For this reason, biometric recognition technologies are spreading that evaluate physical or behavioral traits of the person, such as the fingerprint or the face, acquired through sensors. Biometric systems digitize the user's biometric trait and produce a representation, called a template, which summarizes the unique and constant characteristics of the trait analyzed with respect to the individual who possesses it. The template of an individual, stored on a document or in an archive, is then used during the subsequent recognition phases, comparing the stored templates with the acquired representation of a person undergoing verification. The biometric system decides whether the recognition took place using a similarity measure between the acquired template and those present in the archive.

The performance of a biometric system can vary greatly depending on the biometric trait employed and the level of cooperation required from users. The choice of the biometric trait to be used for specific applications is based on an accurate analysis of the operational and security requirements, obviously taking into consideration the laws on the protection of personal data.

Blockchain and Distributed Ledger

Distributed Ledger (DLT) technology, or blockchain, is the technology used for cryptocurrencies. Let's speak about cryptocurrencies, one of the possible applications of this technology which, using public key cryptography and consensus algorithms, allows to maintain a distributed database of transactions ensuring verifiability, irreversibility and integrity.

There are two categories of DLT platforms: unpermissioned (open) and permissioned (regulated). The first, of which Bitcoin is the best-known example, is maintained by public nodes, and is accessible to anyone. The second involves only authorized nodes and therefore allows faster, safer and more convenient transactions.

Many countries and more than 90 central banks are investing in the adoption of DLT; it is strategic for analyzing the opportunities, risks and challenges related to the adoption of a national DLT infrastructure. A national blockchain (open or regulated) opens up Research and Innovation challenges: from control in the monetary field, to services for the PA and management of digital rights and patent protection; from innovations in electronic voting and distribution chains.

Quantum technologies

The development of quantum technologies has laid the foundations for creating new intrinsically secure communication systems using quantum cryptography, and in particular the quantum distribution of cryptographic keys (Quantum Key Distribution, QKD), which, using the properties of light at the quantum level, allows us to reveal in real time, the presence of attacks and violations of the communication channel, and thus guarantee the security of transmission. QKD consists in the generation of cryptographic keys, shared only between the transmitter and the receiver by transmitting single photons through conventional and unprotected communication channels (for example, optical fibers or in free space).

The cryptographic keys, whose security is guaranteed by the laws of physics, can then be used to encrypt messages between two users, or for other cryptographic protocols.

Quantum technologies are a strategic technology for countries and it is therefore essential that it enhances its scientific and technological capabilities in this sector in order to limit, if not eliminate, its dependence on foreign countries and companies in such a strategic field.

In this regard, it is necessary to develop and test new technologies in the field, and connect them with the most advanced classic techniques of security and data protection.

Technologies to protect

The cybersecurity strategy also contemplates the tools and actions necessary to protect some key technologies, such as wireless communications, cloud services, the functional logic of the systems and, also in the perspective of Enterprise 4.0, IoT systems, industrial control systems and robots.

Wireless communications and 5G systems

The 5G network includes not only the cellular network but also the fixed network, providing services with better performance parameters, by several orders of magnitude compared to current solutions; is characterized by radically new technical solutions, including the implementation in software of complex and critical network functions, now implemented in hardware and the division of the network into slices, each of which provides a subset of users with an autonomous virtual network, capable of meeting specific needs, in an overall framework that sees coexistence within the network of different organizations (multi tenancy).The combination of these characteristics profoundly changes the network security problems.

Cloud

The cloud paradigm certainly offers economic benefits and flexibility in the use of resources. However, the problem of security in cloud environments is a major concern for companies and public organizations that want to move their services, applications and sensitive data to this mode.

The cloud paradigm is based on the principle of delegating the management of infrastructures, data and applications to a third party. This delegation makes part of the system inaccessible and therefore impossible not only to verify the correct application of the envisaged policies, but in some cases also simply to specify the security policy to be adopted with due precision. Normally, even the advanced protection policies of cloud providers are inaccessible to users and above all, not monitored. And so, the guarantee that local regulatory constraints are respected can also become an insurmountable problem. The main challenge for the correct adoption of the cloud passes through the construction of methods and techniques that define and verify the security level of an IT system that uses cloud services within it. The development of security metrics that make it possible to quantitatively evaluate an offer of services of this kind represents one of the most felt challenges from the users' point of view.

Internet of Things

IoT devices are now very widely used because they both improve the quality of the services offered by the equipment in which they are inserted, and allow the creation of new ones. However, their diffusion has dramatically increased the so-called attack surface, introducing in fact new vulnerabilities that can have serious consequences for users, if not prevented and treated in a specific way. This phenomenon is particularly felt today also in the industrial sector where, thanks also to the incentives made available by the various development plans of Impresa 4.0, the spread of IoT devices has reached significant levels.

Industrial Control System

Today, in the industrial field, there is a high level of integration between Information Technology (IT) and Operational Technology (OT). This evolutionary process, the bearer of new functionalities and services, has brought out the need to increase the safety and resilience of industrial control systems (ICS).

Among the aspects to be taken into account in the design and development of security solutions for these systems, particular attention must be paid to the difference between the life time of an ICS system and that of a cybersecurity system. Typically, in fact, while the life time of an ICS system, based on technologies designed and developed for a specific domain, is of the order of 10-15 years, that of a cybersecurity component is much lower, on average of the order of 3-5 years. This difference represents an extremely critical factor when planning the updating and maintenance of ICS systems, due to the stringent requirements of availability and reliability imposed by these systems.

Robot

Robotics today is going beyond its classic boundaries and, from an automatic system mainly used in the industrial and automation world, it is hybridizing with technologies such as Cloud Computing, Artificial Intelligence and IoT.

As regards the cybersecurity aspects, in addition to the security problems deriving from the physical actions of the robot (seen as a device capable of directly performing mechanical actions in the physical world without direct and continuous control by a human operator), a further aspect to be considered concerns the fact that the ability to autonomous movement can also be instrumental to the acquisition of data and information through mobile sensors, with potential risks for the protection of information and personal data. The spread of robots therefore poses a series of interdisciplinary challenges that involve, in addition to the scientific and technological sphere, also the sociological and legal one.

As far as the sociological and judicial sphere is concerned, Italy, like many other countries, is still devoid of regulations governing the use of robots and autonomous devices. For example, it is currently illegal to fly autonomous drones unsupervised.

In general, there is still no in-depth understanding of the criticality profiles introduced by possible cyber-attacks in different areas from both a technical and social point of view.

CYBERSECURITY AND CYBERWAR IN 2021

After this review, we believe it is useful to make some recommendations to policy makers regarding the necessary steps to adequately respond to the challenge of digital transformation. To do this it is necessary to face the challenges at different levels.

The recommendations we make are certainly not intended to be exhaustive, but touch upon two points that we consider essential for a correct implementation of a cyber security policy at national level:

- the development of a national cyber ecosystem that sees government, industry and research united and coordinated to make the country resilient to new cyber-attacks that can directly impact our values and our democracy, as well as our prosperity

- an extraordinary plan to address the lack of skills in this sector, both through strengthening the training and research capacity of universities and through the development of policies to combat forced intellectual emigration

A network of cyber-attack defense centers

The defense of a sovereign state against cyber-attacks, perpetrated by increasingly structured and articulated criminal organizations, requires the creation of a national cyber eco-system which, thanks to the contribution of different subjects and actors, supports the implementation of the national cyber policy. The backbone of this ecosystem will consist of a solid network of centers of competence of various types and types that will revolve around the National

Center for Research and Development in Cybersecurity. In particular, the Center must be the reference point for a constellation of other Territorial Competence Centers in Cybersecurity, distributed throughout the territory with the value of metropolitan, regional or interregional cities and by a set of Vertical Centers of Competence in Cybersecurity.

The National Cybersecurity Research and Development Center will be able to constitute one of the basic pillars of the whole process of implementation of the National Plan for cyber protection and information security. This Center, characterized by a centralized, multidisciplinary structure, with an adequate critical mass, partly governmental and partly linked to the world of public and private research, has as its main task the research, development of platforms, adequate architectural solutions and applications and the implementation of actions of various kinds, aimed at the national interest. The Center will obviously also have the task of assisting policymakers and various public stakeholders in the activities of analysis, scientific research, development, technological scouting and systems engineering, taking into account the international scene.

The Center must be able to attract public and private (national) researchers and investors to develop cutting-edge research on topics of strategic interest for the country in the cyber sector. In this regard, it is desirable that agile and flexible mechanisms are defined and made operational as a matter of urgency to allow researchers and professors of universities and public research bodies to obtain temporary secondment at the Center, without penalties either for seconded staff or for respective institutions of origin. Following the example of the US Federally Funded Research and Development Centers (FFRDC), the Center will have to be the spearhead of national cyber research, coordinating with other research centers present, and taking action to implement the necessary synergies with similar centers in the countries with which the historically collaborates.

The Territorial Centers of Competence in Cybersecurity must be characterized by at least two well-defined objectives relating to support for the local economy and administration, and to raise awareness among citizens. For the economic-administrative aspects, these territorial centers will have to help businesses and the local communities. They will do this by taking care of technology transfer, training, consultancy and providing support for the protection of know - how and physical and virtual assets, and useful tools to improve the offer and competitiveness. These centers will also be able to manage local cybersecurity observatories to share information on attacks between different entities, ensuring due confidentiality, and will be able to contribute to the identification and management of research and technology transfer projects of local strategic interest.

The Vertical Centers of Competence in Cybersecurity will have to respond to the needs of specific market sectors, such as, for example, energy, transport, health and financial markets. The various actors will be able to use the vertical centers, on the one hand, to respond to the need expressed

CYBERSECURITY AND CYBERWAR

IN 2021

by the various sectors to have ad hoc centers for the development of dedicated and specific activities for the domain and, on the other, to ensure the sharing of information through exchange and analysis tables. In the context of cybersecurity, the sharing of information is in fact the basis of any defense strategy; having timely, complete and reliable information enables more informed decisions and accelerates protection actions, as well as actions of detection, reaction, containment and recovery in times of crisis.

The complex mosaic necessary to support the national cyber policy also requires other pieces, which are already included in the National Plan for cyber protection and IT security. We refer to three structures specifically: The National Cryptography Laboratory, the Cyber Range network and the Assessment and Certification Center. The first, which will have to work in close connection with the National Research and Development Center to best combine theory and practice, will serve to bring together the mathematical knowledge of our academies and the long tradition of our military apparatuses in the cryptography sector. The second coordinates virtual polygons dedicated to the training of professionals in the sector, consisting of controlled environments and systems that lend themselves to a wide variety of uses, such as individual training and updating in cybersecurity, training and assessment of skills of teams of operators by carrying out exercises, evaluating and developing new defense tactics and techniques. The third party must instead have the dual purpose of assessing the safety of the products and devices to be installed within the national critical infrastructures and of issuing safety certifications for the products.

An extraordinary plan for training, research and employment

To be implemented, the projects and actions we have proposed require a considerable workforce in terms of technicians, engineers, experts and researchers, distributed throughout the territory. This requires starting an extraordinary plan as soon as possible to retain as many cybersecurity-related skills as possible and to train even more. Some projections predict a global skills shortage of 3.5 million experienced cyber security personnel, and many international organizations are organizing to address the problems associated with this gap. We recall, for example, the initiative of the city of New York which, through a strategic public-private investment plan, aims to "grow the IT security workforce, help companies drive innovation and build networks and common spaces".

Safety-related professionals have a global market and we often find ourselves competing with companies that offer far better working conditions. The flight from this industry to seize important wage opportunities and the poor creation of professional figures adequate to the need make the skills deficit even more critical. Furthermore, we must create the conditions to bring our best brains back into science and business in the security sector.

CYBERSECURITY AND CYBERWAR IN 2021

At the moment, the number of professional figures produced by our universities is too low also due to the low number of professors present in this sector, which in fact prevents both the activation of new degree courses in cybersecurity in many universities and the development of significant research activities. In order to reach a level of workforce adequate to the needs of the country in the shortest possible time, we hope that, as happened in the past for other areas, for example for chemistry in the 1960s, the strategic importance of the cybersecurity sector will be recognized and launched in an extraordinary plan for the recruitment of researchers and university professors who deal with information security and, in general, with digital transformation in all its components: legal, economic and above all technological. Only significant extraordinary action can increase the speed of creation of the necessary critical mass.

Investing in cyber security training and training provides a unique answer to many problems in the country and becomes indispensable in the context of the progressive digitalization promoted by the Enterprise 4.0 plan. Training the new generations will trigger a virtuous process in which the management class and technicians of the future will have the skills, cultural background and operational skills necessary to deal with the technological and scientific challenges that will change our lives in the coming decades, developing the initiatives necessary to face the continuous changes and the related risks that await us in the future.

Leaders in Cybersecurity

Imperva's top leaders in cybersecurity; The top officials in Information Security

This was revealed by a list of Imperva, one of the leading companies in the sector with over 4,500 customers and 500 partners in more than 90 countries. The list includes the top influencers in terms of opinion and thinking in online safety. The goal for all of them is to make the internet safer. The first is Eve Adams, Senior Technical Recruiting Strategist at Centro. His job is to build technical teams specialized in countering cyber threats. He also deals with open-source technologies, NLP languages, Information Security and transparency. Followed by Dimple Ahluwalia, who has been with IBM since 2007. He is currently an officer in the security services division of the giant, he manages security consulting and systems integration in North America. In third position is Aloria: a security engineer at Tumblr. In his spare time, he teaches at the Computer Science and Engineering Department of the NYU Tandon School of Engineering.

There is no shortage of Cyber lawyers and authors

The fourth female cybersecurity influencer is Christina Ayiotis, a well-known cyber security lawyer. Today she is a consultant and lawyer for Cyber Sabbatical. In fifth position is Stephanie Balaouras, vice president and director of research at Forrester Research. She is a high-tech analyst specializing in IT risk, security, infrastructure and operations. In sixth place is Ann Barron-DiCamillo, CTO of Strategic Cyber Ventures. Violet Blue is seventh. She is an author on technology, privacy, and security culture across multiple media. She is an activist for promoting the role of women in the technology sector. Furthermore, she is committed to spreading awareness among people about the risks deriving from cyberspace. Kate Brew, content manager at Alien Vault, ranks eighth, specializes in information security. Joyce Brocaglia is ninth, she is the founder of the Executive Woman's Forum. In tenth place is Lesley Carhart, specialized in Digital forensics.

Also present are the top security of social platforms

Imperva's list of top female cybersecurity leaders cites Brandie Claborn, head of corporate communications for Intel Security; Diana-Lynn Contesti, expert in solving problems related to the security arena; Eleanor Dallaway editor and editor of Infosecurity Magazine; Anita D'Amico, experimental psychologist and CEO at Code Dx , Inc ; Mary-Ann Davidson, Chief Security Officer at Oracle Corporation; Erin Egan, Vice President and Chief Privacy Officer in Policy at Facebook since 2011; Limor Elbaz , founder and CEO of Peerlyst ; Marisa Fagan, cybersecurity culture expert and Senior Manager Secure Engineering at Salesforce , as well as founder of InfoSec Mentors; Debra J. Farber, one of the heads of Visa's Global Public Policy Department; Lisa Foreman-Jiggetts , founder of the Women's Society of Cyberjutsu Deborah Frincke, director of research at the National Security Agency (NSA).

Also present are consultants and university teachers

Prachi Gupta is the Director of Engineering at LinkedIn while Jenn Henley leads security at Facebook. Jessy Irwin, on the other hand, works at both Mercury Public Affairs and AgileBits, Inc. She deals with security awareness and training for non- technical audiences. Cecily Joseph is the chief diversity officer of Symantec Corp; Juliette Kayyem was Assistant Secretary for Intergovernmental Affairs of the Homeland Security Department in the Obama administration. Limor S Kessem is an Executive Security Advisor with IBM and works with cybersecurity researchers. Mischel Kwon is president of MKA Cyber, specialized in technical defensive security, security operations and information assurance, he also teaches at George Washington University, where he also oversees the institute's Cyber Defense Lab. Shannon Lietz leads a DevSecOps team supporting Red Team Mondays, Blue Team Intelligence and Cloud Security Engineering at Intuit. Tamara McCleary is the CEO of Thulium.co and one of the top 50 social media influencers in the industry.

Others are leaders among industry journalists and cryptographers

Reporter Elinor Mills is now Vice Resident of Content and Media Strategy with the Bateman Group. Allison Miller, on the other hand, is a product strategist on Google's security team. Jennifer Minella is Vice President of Engineering and CISO Consulting at Carolina Advanced Digital Inc. She is also a consultant to several US government agencies and training institutes, as well as to Fortune 100 and 500. She has become one of the 10 top power players and influencers in the IT security. Marie Moe is a researcher and specialist in cryptography and information security, working at SINTEF Information and Communication Technology in Trondheim. In addition, associated with the Norwegian University of Science and Technology. Christina Morillo is an identity and access management expert. She works for several companies and is the co-founder of We Are Women of Color in Tech. Katie Moussouris, founder and CEO of Luta Security, helps companies and governments defend against cyber threats.

Women at the top also in malware research

Wendy Nather is director of research at the Retail Cyber Intelligence Sharing Center in Austin. Bev Robb is an IT consultant and is known on the web as Teksquisite, working to keep social media safe. Amanda Rousseau is a malware research specialist at Endgame Inc.; Joanna Rutkowska is the founder and CEO of Invisible Things Lab. Sherry Ryan is Vice President and Chief Information Security Officer at Juniper

Networks. Runa Sandvik is the director of Information Security at the New York Times and technical advisor to the Freedom of the Press Foundation. Additionally, she is a member of the Black Hat Dollars peer review board. Masha Sedova is Senior Director of Trust Engagement at Salesforce.

Finally, there are the activists for the promotion of gender equality in cybersecurity

Parisa Tabriz manages Chrome engineering teams and helps make the operating system secure and stable. Julie Talbot-Hubbard is Senior Vice President and Head of Information Security Operations at SunTrust. She previously held a similar position at Symantec. Sandra Toms is RSA vice president and curator of its annual global conference. Georgia Weidman is the founder and CTO of SheVirah, Inc. and is also a consultant to the Digital Citizens Alliance. Finally, Tarah Wheeler is a hacker and website security Czar. She is currently the Principal Security Advocate and Senior Director of Engineering, Website Security at Symantec. She was co-founder of Fizzmint and LadyCoders , LLC., An organization that promotes gender equality in the tech community.

1. Nicole Eagan, Darktrace

As Co- Chief Executive Officer of Darktrace, Nicole Eagan has established a computer security company as a global leader in cyber defense AI. Eagan introduced disruptive machine learning for businesses of all sizes, earning industry-wide recognition as an AI thought leader.

Creating the market for autonomous response, Darktrace stops a cyber threat from causing damage every three seconds with its AI algorithms. Eagan has led the company since 2014, positioning the company to garner a loyal customer base while earning a $2 billion valuation. Her work doesn't stop at improving cybersecurity, but continues as Eagan leads internal and external efforts in the technology sector. This starts with Darktrace, which maintains roughly equal numbers of male and female employees in an industry where women make up only about 20% of the workforce.

2. Lisa Schreiber, Forcepoint

As Chief Customer Success Officer of Forcepoint, Lisa Schreiber is responsible for overseeing the ability of Global's customers, the overall customer experience from acquisition to retention. With over 30 years of experience, Schreiber is celebrated as a prominent leader in world-class customer experience. At Forcepoint, she is instrumental in the company's reputation as a true strategic cybersecurity partner for businesses around the world. Prior to Forcepoint, Schreiber was vice president of North American Customer Success and Support Services for Oracle and held various executive positions at Golden Gate Software, Schwab, US Trust Corporation and Apple. While at Oracle, Schreiber led the success of Oracle's 200 largest corporate clients. Schreiber is also a member of the Board of Visitors of the University of Pittsburgh School of Computing and Information. She also regularly speaks to high school and college students about the global reach and importance of STEM careers.

3. Jaya Baloo, Avast

As Avast Software's current Chief Information Security Officer, Jaya Baloo is a respected authority on cybersecurity. With over 20 years of experience, Baloo is an expert in a wide range of topics, including forensic interception, mass surveillance and encryption. Prior to joining Avast, she held various roles, including the head of legal wiretapping at Verizon, the chief information security officer at KPN Telecom, and the technology security specialist overseeing fraud and revenue guarantee at France Telecom. Today, Jaya is a valued member of the Avast team, a recognized leader in digital security products with over 400 million online users. The security leader balances her position at Avast with being a faculty member of Singularity University. She is also a notable expert in quantum computing, which led Jaya to become a quantum ambassador for KPN Telecom and a vice president of the Commission's Quantum Flagship Strategic Advisory Board.

4. Hue Harguindeguy, Guardian Analytics

Hue Harguindeguy was appointed Co-CEO and Chief Financial Officer of Guardian Analytics in 2016. However, her experience does not end in the financial sector, but extends to international business structures, human resources practices, and labor immigration and welfare requirements around the world. Founded in 2005, the Mount View , California-based company has been at the forefront of leveraging machine learning and advanced big data analytics to mitigate the risk of fraud and stop sophisticated criminal attacks targeting retail customers, commercial and corporate banking: digital bank fraud detection for mobile and online devices, real-time payment fraud detection for wire transfer and ACH anti-money laundering solutions which include link analysis and FinCEN reports , which meet AML compliance requirements on a single platform, thus simplifying the case filing process.

5. Sri Subramanian, Netskope

Sri Subramanian spent just over a year at Netskope as Senior Director of Product Management, but her achievements are virtually endless. In particular, she was instrumental in creating a secure coprocessor that was installed on every Intel motherboard, the highest-rated SSL VPN, the most widely used identity management product, as well as the first set of products on Oracle Cloud. Founded in 1990, the Santa Clara-based company is recognized as a leading cybersecurity company, helping the world's largest companies use the cloud without sacrificing security. Netskope Security Cloud helps organizations reap the benefits of increased employee collaboration and productivity. She was the founder and CEO of Evolv.ng, one of the fastest-adopted high school advisor platforms that allows counselors to provide personalized college admission directions to students on their phones.

6. Evgeniya Naumova, Kaspersky

Kaspersky is one of the world's largest private providers of endpoint cybersecurity solutions, as vice president of Kaspersky's global sales network, Evgeniya Naumova is responsible for sales operations across all business segments, including consumers and B2B. Prior to joining Kaspersky, Naumova oversaw corporate sales at Dr.Web and was director of international sales at Protection Technology.

7. Tia Hopkins, Hear

Tia Hopkins is Vice President of Global Sales Engineering at the cybersecurity firm eSentire. That's perfect considering she is an avid cybersecurity enthusiast, particularly interested in how security relates to humanity. The Waterloo, Ontario-based company, founded in 2001, is the largest provider of tracking and managed response (MDR), which protects organizations from evolving cyber threats that technology alone cannot intercept. Here, Hopkins focuses on guiding her team to provide pre-sales engineering solutions. Prior to joining eSentire, Hopkins held various technology roles at Zones Inc., Bessinger Technology, KapTechnology and Verizon. He balances his role with that of a part-time professor of Cybersecurity at Yeshiva University.

She is also passionate about engaging more women in cybersecurity while promoting awareness of gender inequalities in the industry with organizations such as Leading Cyber Ladies and the Women's Society of Cyberjutsu.

8. Sarah Ashburn, Attivo Networks

Since joining Attivo Networks as Vice President of Sales, Sarah Ashburn has built the North American sales department for Attivo solutions. This includes resolving robotic threat (BOT) and advanced persistent threats (APT) vulnerabilities on networks and data centers. She has grown businesses at all stages, from startups to established brands, and has significant talent in developing security market sales for Fortune 2000. Prior to joining Attivo Networks, Ashburn held sales leadership roles at VMware, Symantec and VERITAS Technologies. Founded in 2011, the California-based cybersecurity firm of Fremont is now a leader in deception technology as well as providing unique and complementary solutions to an organization's existing security infrastructure.

9. Yael Ben Arie, SafeBreach

As SafeBreach's Vice President of Research and Development and CEO of SafeBreach Israel, Yael Ben Arie leads the company's product development for a category-defining cybersecurity platform that handles thousands of hackings and attacking methods at scale across multiple clouds and operating systems, to help enterprises improve their security status and reduce business risk. Previously, she led the cybersecurity, data, machine learning and cloud security research teams at Trusteer (IBM). Her focus at IBM / Trusteer was to stop sophisticated cyber threats against global banks and help banks fight online fraud. Prior to her working career, Yael, a trained military pilot, served in the Israeli Air Force as an operations officer in a combat squadron. Yael is also a leadership consultant for the "she codes" community where she mentors young women in the IT industry. She holds a BS in Computer Science and Math with honors from Hebrew University.

10. Leslie Jones, Coalfire

An experienced HR professional, Leslie Jones brings over 20 years of experience to her role as Chief Human Resources Officer at Coalfire. She has been consistently praised for her leadership in developing an inclusive culture in the company that puts employees at ease. Jones worked with her team to expand Coalfire's values, known as "The Coalfire Way", to include a new commitment to "working together as one". In her team, she emphasizes honesty, connectivity and progress. Jones' role encompasses recruiting, training and development programs, compensation and benefits, talent management and building a vibrant corporate culture. Prior to joining Coalfire, Jones was Vice President of Human Resources at Benefitfocus, Director of Human Resources at Blackbaud, and spent nine years at Sun Microsystems as a Senior Human Resources Manager and HR Business Partner.

11. Selena Proctor, Onapsis

As Vice President of Strategic Initiatives of Onapsis, Selena Proctor guides the execution of strategic goals to increase global awareness of the company in the market. She has over eleven years of cybersecurity marketing experience as well as a strong background in demand generation. Headquartered in Boston, Massachusetts, Onapsis provides actionable information, secure modification, automated governance, and continuous monitoring for mission- critical systems from well-known vendors such as SAP, Oracle and leading SaaS platforms. Over the past seven years, Selena has held various roles at Onapsis, starting as director of marketing programs, then vice president of marketing before becoming vice president of strategic initiatives and chief of staff for the CEO. Her unique vision was celebrated for directly enabling awareness of the Onapsis brand in the market.

12. Sagit Manor, Nyotron

Sagit Manor is the CEO of Nyotron, a cybersecurity company that doesn't study past attacks or hacker behavior. It was a disruptive system that overturned every other cybersecurity principle by postulating that "stopping threats has [nothing] to do with knowing them." Manor reflects the company's enthusiasm and confidence in their unconventional yet revolutionary process. Her background is in finance and the payments industry, Prior to Nyotron, Manor held roles at Ernst & Young, as chief financial officer at Lipman and as vice president and chief financial officer at Verifone. Sagit also led an IPO on NASDAQ, as well as several strategic acquisitions before joining the cybersecurity firm in 2017.

CYBERSECURITY AND CYBERWAR IN 2021

LEADING COMPANIES IN CYBERSECURITY

Cybersecurity 500 https://cybersecurityventures.com/cybersecurity-500/ - 18-6-2018

#	Company	Cybersecurity Sector	Corporate HQ
1	Herjavec Group	Information Security Services	Toronto, Canada
2	KnowBe4	Security Awareness Training	Clearwater FL
3	CyberArk	Privileged Access Security	Petach-Tikva, Israel
4	Raytheon Cyber	Cyber Security Services	Waltham MA
5	Cisco	Threat Protection & Network Security	San Jose CA
6	IBM Security	Enterprise IT Security Solutions	Waltham MA
7	Microsoft	Datacenter to Endpoint Protection	Redmond WA
8	Amazon Web Services	Cloud-Powered Security	Seattle WA
9	FireEye	Advanced Threat Protection	Milpitas CA
10	Lockheed Martin	Cybersecurity Solutions & Services	Bethesda MD
11	Check Point Software	Unified Threat Management	Tel Aviv, Israel
12	RSA	Intelligence Driven Security	Bedford MA
13	Symantec	Endpoint, Cloud & Mobile Security	Mountain View CA
14	BAE Systems	Cybersecurity Risk Management	Surrey, UK
15	Booz Allen	Cybersecurity Solutions & Services	New York City NY
16	Palo Alto Networks	Threat Detection & Prevention	Santa Clara CA
17	Rapid7	Security Data & Analytics Solution	Boston MA
18	Proofpoint	Security-as-a-Service	Sunnyvale CA
19	Splunk	Big Data Security	San Francisco CA
20	SecureWorks	Managed Security Services	Atlanta GA
21	Optiv	Information Security Services	Denver CO
22	Intel	Hardware Enabled Security	Santa Clara CA
23	Carbon Black	Endpoint & Server Security Platform	Waltham MA
24	KPMG	Cyber Risk Management	London, UK
25	Northrop Grumman	Cyber & Homeland Security Services	McLean VA

The 4 big names in cybersecurity

The ranking changes as rapidly as malwares spread, it includes many well-known names in the technological and financial fields: IBM, Cisco, Symantec, Deloitte, PwC, Kaspersky Lab, Intel, BlackBerry, Accenture, KPMG ...

And here are the Fabulous Four of the moment:

1st - HERJAVEC GROUP - Toronto, Canada - Group founded in 2003 by Robert Herjavec, histrionic and controversial IT entrepreneur called "shark", has its core business in information security, making a rapid climb among the companies in the technology sector of North America.

It offers compliance, risk management, incident response (including intrusion and hacker attacks) and network issues, data recovery and protection services. In addition to Toronto, it has offices in New York, Reading (UK) and Sydney, Australia. It employs about 300 people and would have increased its turnover from 400 thousand to over 140 million dollars in the first 12 years of operation.

2nd - KNOWBE4 - Tampa Bay, USA - Specialized in corporate training on phishing and ransomware, works with 18,000 organizations worldwide and was in 6th place in this ranking last year alone. The CEO, Kevin Mitnick, is an internationally recognized cybersecurity expert.

The company, after 18 consecutive quarters of growth, benefited from an investment of $30 million last year from bank Goldman Sachs. The bank vice president himself, Hans Sherman, has joined the board of KnowBe4. The company now ranks 231 in the annual ranking of the 5,000 fastest growing companies in America. And it recently acquired Popcorn Training, a company based in Johannesburg and Cape Town, South Africa.

3rd - CYBERARK - Petah Tikva, Israel - Listed on NASDAQ, it has offices around the world and the US headquarters in Newton, Massachusetts. Over $ 260 million in revenue in 2017, and a jump of 12 places in this ranking, have further turned the spotlight on this Israeli company.

Originally specialized in the protection of sensitive information for banks and insurance companies. It now also deals with real-time automatic threat detection and damage containment. Its technology is used primarily in the financial services, energy, retail and healthcare sectors. It has over 3,800 customers, including nearly 30% from Forbes' Global 2000 list and more than half from Fortune 100.

4th - RAYTHEON CYBER - Waltham, USA - It is part of a group of 63,000 employees operating in the defense and military supplies sector, in close relationship with the American government. It specializes in the management, analysis and security of data, protection, research, evaluation and contrast of cyber threats. The estimated turnover of the entire group is $24.6 billion.

Cybersecurity, US companies trump worldwide expenditure

Online security is a priority for 20% of UK business leaders, compared with 41% of those US and 30% globally. Mark Hughes (BT Security): "We need to invest in training"

CYBERSECURITY AND CYBERWAR
IN 2021

20% of UK business leaders considers information security a top priority, compared with 41% registered in the US and 30% globally. Emerging from research commissioned by BT and conducted by Vanson Bourne in October 2013 on a sample of 500 IT managers from medium and large companies in 7 countries.

The aim of the research is "to probe the attitude towards information security and the capacity of action of those responsible", and highlights "the backwardness of Companies dollars expenditure in comparison to their US counterparts."

"Just over half (58%) of UK companies are able to calculate the return on investment (ROI) from cybersecurity measures, compared with 90% of US companies. But that's not all: in the US, 86% of managers and decision-makers participating in training courses of cybersecurity, while in Sterling the figure is only 44%. "

"The different levels of operational readiness depend on the attitude adopted towards threats - the company states - On a global scale, unintentional internal threats (e.g. accidental data loss) are what worries the most: they represent a serious threat for 65% of IT managers. In UK, the percentage drops to 56%, followed by intentional internal threats (53%), hacktivism (48%), organized crime (38%) and hacking with intent of political activism (31%). In the United States, there are 85% of IT managers who consider accidental insider threats a serious threat; followed by intentional internal threats (79%), hacktivism (77%), organized crime (75%), terrorism (72%) and political activism (70%)".

"The research offers an interesting perspective on the changing landscape of cyber threats and the consequent difficulties for companies around the world - says Mark Hughes, CEO of BT Security - Following the enormous spread of employee-owned devices, cloud computing and extranets, the risks of misuse and attacks have multiplied, exposing companies to a myriad of internal and external threats, both intentional and accidental. "

"In response to the constant changes on the threat front - continues Hughes - CEOs and top managers need to invest in cyber security, offering appropriate training tools to employees not only in the IT area.

Strategy and artificial intelligence for a secure Cloud

The more a corporate network opens to the outside, the more production, financial and business data are transferred to the Cloud and the greater the risks for data protection. The cybersecurity is often experienced as a brake to the acceleration of digitization of our business and the widespread use in recent months of digital platforms to access business documents and collaborative working tools, even from personal devices, has increased the level of attention to the safety computer science, but also the vulnerability to possible attacks, if not treated correctly.

However, the problem is not just known, as emerges from the Oracle and Kpmg Cloud Threat Report 2020.

The Oracle and Kpmg survey on Cloud threats, the "Cloud Threat Report", highlights the main challenges in Cloud security worldwide, through the experience and perception that company employees have.

750 IT and cybersecurity managers from private and public companies in North America (USA, Canada), West Europe (UK and France) and Asia Pacific (Australia, Japan, Singapore) were interviewed between December 2019 and January 2020, with the responsibility to evaluate, purchase and manage cyber-security products and services and have a high knowledge of the use of the public cloud by your organization.

What emerges from the research is a high concern (three times as much for the security of one's home network) and a lot of confusion both in the use of security systems and in the integration with internal legacy, i.e. the hardware and software systems already present in the company, and with respect to the so-called "shared responsibility" of the Cloud.

But the process is now unstoppable: almost 90% of companies use SaaS (Software as a Service) services, 76% IaaS (Infrastructure as a Service) and one in two plans to transfer all data to the Cloud within two years. By bringing more and more critical data to the Cloud, however, new "blind spots" have also been created and confusion reigns supreme. The majority of companies (78%), in fact, declare that they use over 50 different security solutions to deal with security problems internally and 37% use over a hundred of them.

Organizations that have detected improperly configured cloud services have encountered over 10 data loss incidents in the past year, and only 8% say they understand the shared responsibility model in cloud security. In particular, in the public cloud, the service provider is responsible for the infrastructure, while applications and data, and related security, are the responsibility of the customer.

In the SaaS model, on the other hand, the Apps are also the responsibility of the provider, but the data remain the property and responsibility of the customer. Thus, 87% of enterprises are counting on the integration of artificial intelligence and machine learning to equip themselves with safer products in the future.

Digital strategy with security first

But it is a product-only problem, or a lack of a network architecture that includes a digital security strategy, with a "Security-first" model, where providers and IT work together, rather than relying on emergency interventions, often implemented too late and causing confusion about each other's responsibilities. The point is that cybersecurity criticalities are not solved automatically with the cloud, they simply move.

CYBERSECURITY AND CYBERWAR IN 2021

In fact, 75% of IT professionals consider the public Cloud to be more secure than their data centers, but 92% do not believe that their company is prepared to protect data and applications in the Cloud. 69% of companies, for example, say their CISOs (Chief Information Security Officers) were only involved after a cybersecurity incident in Cloud projects, and most would still want them with more Cloud security skills.

Now, more than half have hired the Business Information Security Officer (BISO), a new figure who works with the CISO, precisely to migrate the culture of security into the business and obtain the necessary strategic investments.

Global co-leader and US leader cybersecurity services of KPMG LLP, suggests that companies have accelerated the transfer of workloads and sensitive data to the cloud platform to support the new working model and optimize costs. This transformation is generating vulnerabilities and new risks. Thus, in order to manage the increased threat level, it is essential that the CISO integrate security into the Cloud migration process and implementation strategies, maintaining constant communication with the company.

Yes, artificial intelligence, but with a strategic approach to the Cloud

Adds Steve Daheb, senior vice president of Oracle Cloud: «In the last two years, bringing critical information to the Cloud has proved to be a promising choice, but it has created a fairly 'monstrous' mix of security tools and processes, with frequent and costly problems. of configuration errors and data loss. However, progress is being made. The adoption of tools that use machine learning to close the skill gap is on the IT shopping list for the immediate future ".

And he concludes: "At the same time, top management is working to bring all business lines to adopt a corporate culture that puts safety first".

THE 10 BEST ACQUISITIONS OF CYBERSECURITY COMPANIES

Some of the most exciting investments, acquisitions and strategic moves made in the industry by cybersecurity firms throughout 2018.

Cybercrime is currently the biggest threat to businesses and users, and cybercrime is estimated to cost the world $6 trillion annually by 2021, up from $3 trillion in 2015.

In an effort to minimize cybercrime, companies in cyberspace are undoubtedly doing their utmost to combat cyber threats. According to Markets and Markets, the market for cybersecurity solutions and services (including IAM tools, encryption, UTM, antivirus and antimalware, firewalls, IDS / IPS, disaster recovery and DDoS mitigation) will hit approximately $153 billion in 2018, with the expectation that this figure will rise to more than $248 billion in 2023.

CYBERSECURITY AND CYBERWAR
IN 2021

Impressive numbers, highlighted by the numerous investment acquisitions that large cybersecurity companies have made over the year.

Amazon

Given its size and scale, everything Amazon does in the cybersecurity space is significant. The acquisition of the company by Sqrrl in January 2018 was noteworthy because it highlighted Amazon's confidence in the effectiveness of threat hunting as a means to quickly identify and mitigate cyber threats.

In recent years, Amazon has also led the way with other security initiatives designed to address corporate concerns about moving sensitive workloads to the cloud. The most significant of these efforts is work on encryption and the use of artificial intelligence to address security issues. An Amazon unit called Automated Reasoning Group (ARG) has done much of the work in applying automation to reduce cloud security risks for business.

Cisco

Cisco is rapidly emerging as a significant player in the cybersecurity industry through acquisitions, such as its purchase of Duo Security in August for $2.35 billion. The purchase should position Cisco as a strong competitor in the multifactor authentication space - a market that analyst Markets & Markets expects to exceed $12.5 billion by 2022.

Duo adds to the growing number of security companies that Cisco has acquired in recent years. Others include Sourcefire, Lancope, and ThreatGRID. Technologies from these vendors and Cisco's homegrown products drove growing cybersecurity revenues for Cisco at a time when growth in the company's core router and switch markets was slowing. For the fiscal year ending 2018, Cisco posted security revenue of nearly $2.4 billion, up 9% from the previous year.

Claroty

Industrial control systems (ICS) security provider Claroty received major recognition for its technology this year when an investor union invested in a $60 million funding round within the company in June. The funding round was significant because the investors included several control system vendors and industrial network operators, such as Rockwell Automation, and venture firms backed by companies such as Schneider Electric and Siemens.

Industrial cybersecurity emerged as a major concern this year among the news of greatest interest to critical infrastructure objectives among state-backed threat actors. Claroty is a small, rapidly growing group of security vendors that cater to the growing needs of this market. The seller has raised $93 million to date and claims to have major customers in a variety of critical infrastructure industries, including oil and gas, utilities, chemicals, manufacturing and water.

CYBERSECURITY AND CYBERWAR IN 2021

Darktrace

Darktrace raised $50 million in a funding round this year that valued the UK-based company at $1.65 billion. The funding, led by private equity firm Vitruvian Partners, was the latest recognition of investor confidence in Darktrace and its AI-based malicious intrusion detection and response technology.

As of July 2017, Darktrace had raised $75 million in an investment round led by Insight Venture Partners, with the participation of several other existing investors in the company. A year earlier, Darktrace had raised $65 million in growth equity funds from KKR and other investment firms.

Since 2015, investors have invested at least $230 million in financing across multiple investment rounds. In the process, Darktrace 's market valuation went from $80 million just three years ago to the current value of 1.65 billion. The funding has helped the security vendor accelerate its momentum in various markets and increase its headcount by 60% to 750 employees worldwide over the past 12 months. The company reported 100% revenue growth in the past year, but did not disclose the actual amount.

Intel

Intel in June hired cybersecurity veteran Window Snyder as the security manager of the Intel Platform Security division. The move was perceived by many as a sign of Intel's greater focus on safety after a year in which the researchers found several critical flaws in Intel microprocessors, particularly vulnerable, Specter and Meltdown.

Prior to Intel, Snyder was head of security at Fastly, and before that he held key roles in strengthening security at Apple, Mozilla and Microsoft.

As a CSO at Intel, Snyder is tasked with ensuring that the chip maker maintains a competitive security product roadmap and remains committed to the security ecosystem.

McAfee

This year, McAfee entered the fast-growing cloud security market by purchasing Skyhigh Networks, a cloud access security broker (CASB) technology provider. The purchase gave McAfee access to a range of technologies designed to give businesses greater visibility and control over user activity and devices across software, Internet, and service platforms.

McAfee also acquired VPN provider TunnelBear this year in a move designed to strengthen the provider's capabilities on the consumer side of its business. The two acquisitions gave the security vendor the opportunity to expand and grow their endpoint security technologies in the cloud.

McAfee currently has annual revenues of $2.6 billion and is looking for more acquisitions.

CYBERSECURITY AND CYBERWAR IN 2021

Oracle

Oracle has quietly developed its security features in an effort to help companies using Oracle's cloud services to better protect their applications and workloads from cyber threats.

In October, at Oracle OpenWorld, the company announced new cloud security features acquired primarily from the purchase of Zenedge last March and Palerra in 2016. The new services include a web application firewall and denial of protection feature service distributed by the purchase of Zenedge and a CASB service based on the Palerra acquisition of Oracle.

Palo Alto Networks

Palo Alto Networks, has made two major acquisitions in the cloud security space.

In March, the security provider announced plans to acquire Evident.io in a $300 million transaction that gave it access to a new set of API-based cloud infrastructure protection features. It later acquired cloud security analytics firm RedLock for $173 million in October.

Proofpoint

With the acquisition of Wombat Security Technologies for $225 million in March, Proofpoint demonstrated a different approach in helping organizations solve one of their biggest security problems: phishing.

Wombat's phishing simulation and security awareness platform is designed to offer businesses a way to educate users about threats.

By combining Wombat's security education platform with its own endpoint protection technologies, Proofpoint currently offers security teams the ability to conduct more realistic phishing simulations aimed at specific end users. The combination of the two technologies has enabled Proofpoint to offer features that enable corporate security teams to investigate and mitigate user-reported phishing attacks faster and to automatically quarantine or reset user accounts.

Red Hat

In October, Red Hat previewed new Ansible integrations designed to give enterprises a way to automate and orchestrate security functions, such as firewalls, intrusion detection systems (IDS), and security information and event management (SIEM). The goal is to enable faster responses to security incidents by coordinating and orchestrating heterogeneous security technologies. Other potential use cases for the technology include searching for threats and suspicious activity.

IBM acquired Red Hat for $34 billion in October. With this agreement Red Hat will join IBM's Hybrid Cloud group, although it will function as a standalone unit. We can't say yet how the acquisition will impact Red Hat's plans for Ansible's advancement. IBM itself has stated that it will

CYBERSECURITY AND CYBERWAR IN 2021

continue the course on all of Red Hat's current projects and plans.

Why is cyber security important to businesses?

" Why is IT security important"? It is something that many are still wondering. In this book I will try to offer you a brief overview of the basic motivations.

"Why is cyber security important?"

The answer may seem simple enough, considering that the number of cyber threats is growing significantly and exponentially.

Consequently, it is not surprising that this is a question that is being asked more and more frequently and the fundamental knowledge that underlies it is something that companies in the sector, professionals and entrepreneurs in general should be aware of.

A little Google search is enough to realize that by now, we are facing a proliferation of cyber-attacks that is causing increasing damage to companies, governments and individuals.

Let's take WannaCry's attacks in May 2017 as a case in point: ransomware has hacked into some 300,000 computers and other digital software in over 150 countries.

Let's talk about what has been called: "the greatest cyber assault of this kind".

Simply put, organizations need to respond to this increased threat by adopting stringent cyber security measures.

In this book I will try to give you the three main answers to the question: "why is cyber security important?" and which illustrate very well why it is such a promising market:

- ❖ the exponential growth in the number of cyber attacks
- ❖ the growing severity of these assaults
- ❖ the amount of money invested by companies in cyber security expenses.

MARKETING AND COMMERCIAL

1. Rising threats

As I said above, the number of cyber security attacks is increasing every year. In the period 2013-2015, the cost of cybercrimes, in the United States alone, quadrupled, reaching figures that are around 400/500 billion dollars during that period.

CYBERSECURITY AND CYBERWAR IN 2021

Every day millions of attacks are developed and then applied.

In a cyber-crime report from Cybersecurity Ventures, the company predicts that the cost of cyber threats will rise by $ 6 trillion annually by 2021, which includes everything:

- ✓ damage and destruction of data,
- ✓ stolen money,
- ✓ loss of productivity,
- ✓ intellectual property theft,
- ✓ misappropriation,
- ✓ fraud,
- ✓ forensic investigations,
- ✓ restoration and deletion of compromised data and systems ...

...just to name a few.

What investors may not know is the growing threat of cyberattacks on medical devices, which is expected to reach $101 billion by 2018.

2. Severity of attacks

However, it is not only the number of cyber security attacks that is increasing, the degree of these attacks is also growing rapidly. According to the PwC (Price Waterhouse Coopers) report on cybersecurity, these attacks are "becoming progressively destructive and target an ever-wider range of information and attack vectors."

Politicians are at risk. The Obama administration proposed a $19 billion budget for cybersecurity. Hillary Clinton's private emails became front page news in the midst of her presidential campaign, underlining the importance of a strong cybersecurity policy.

In May 2017, current President Donald Trump signed an executive order focused on improving cybersecurity in the United States, specifically for the country's infrastructure systems and federal computer networks.

3. Future prospects

Going forward, PwC's 2017 Global Information Security Survey states that 59 percent of Global State of Information Security Survey (GSISS) respondents say "the digitization of their business ecosystems has impacted" their budgets.

As these statistics show, cybersecurity is a very important and commitment-worthy area and companies respond accordingly.

CYBERSECURITY AND CYBERWAR IN 2021

The struggle between growing needs and limited funding is, however, characteristic of the cybersecurity industry. It is therefore essential that companies recognize the importance of cybersecurity and allocate funds accordingly.

We are used to believing that a hacker attacks a computer to destroy it ... with devastating effects (explosions, flames, black holes) quite evident.

In fact, the further we go, the more silent and absolutely transparent the attacks become.

In the information age, the true value lies in data and, for a hacker, it is essential not to be discovered in order to have the opportunity to steal as much information as possible.

At this point the question is:

> "Are you already under attack and continue your life as if nothing had happened?"

Cyber security: how to defend against cyber threats in 2020

Cyber security should be a top priority in every company, and should therefore have a manager appointed by top management. The fragility of the information age we are experiencing requires strong control, adequate tools and trained personnel.

CYBERSECURITY AND CYBERWAR
IN 2021

Cyber security consists in ensuring the integrity, confidentiality and availability of information, a concept translated into English in the acronym ICA (Integrity, Confidentiality and Availability). It represents the ability to defend against or neutralize the effects of incidents such as hard disk failure or cyber-attacks from various types of attackers.

Now we will see how the world of cybersecurity has changed over the years to understand what are the main risks that threaten people and companies, and the main defense tools to set up an effective cybersecurity strategy.

The role of cybersecurity has changed dramatically in recent years. If the first viruses were created and spread almost as a joke, in the eighties hackers attacked systems as a challenge to institutions and demonstration of their abilities, in the nineties we begin to understand that intrusions and tampering of systems create real economic damage.

Laws are created to combat cybercrime, introducing the concept of cyber-crime and the cybersecurity industry blossoms. In the 2000s, the internet provided new means of attack and organization. Organizations like Anonymous and other " hacktivists " see the light, they are driven by political motivations.

Since 2010, on the other hand, increasingly sophisticated attacks have been multiplied by criminal organizations that deploy advanced tools and skills and substantial human resources. Nation-states also create their own attack structures that target companies, political organizations and critical infrastructure in rival countries. With the Advanced and Persistent Threats (APT) begins the era of cyberwarfare, the network war.

In the meantime, the digital revolution touches every private, professional and political activity: cloud, mobile, apps and social networks transform daily life, business models of companies and political communication, while opening everyone up to the risk of theft of sensitive data, blackmail and manipulation of opinions.

Tools such as big data, artificial intelligence and social media allow unscrupulous companies and organizations like Cambridge Analytica to alter election results or polarize companies, while dark organizations infiltrate the cyber infrastructures of countries, political organizations and strategic companies. Lawmakers therefore address the issue of privacy and the protection of critical services, introducing rules such as the GDPR and the NIS directive.

Cyber security in the new digital world

The entry into the field of new, very powerful attackers on the one hand, and the increasing complexity of the tools and applications to be defended, have made the cyber security countermeasures adopted until a few years ago obsolete, which were essentially concentrated in two points:

- Perimeter protection, with firewalls and network security equipment that blocked any attempt to access the corporate network outside;

- Endpoint protection: antivirus and software installed on PCs and servers to protect them from malware.

These defenses continue to represent a first bulwark, but they are no longer enough. People today manage work information on the most disparate devices (smartphones, tablets, computers, wearable devices ...) through different network connections (company network, home line, cell phone, public Wi -Fi ...) and use - sometimes improperly - cloud services for backup, collaboration and file sharing. Each company must therefore build a cyber security strategy that takes into account multiple factors, often using specific tools that must be monitored and coordinated to ensure effective protection. Here are some aspects of cybersecurity to consider.

Critical infrastructure security

Critical infrastructures include physical systems that the company depends on, including the power grid, aqueducts, transportation networks and hospitals. Connecting a power plant to the internet, for example, exposes it to possible cyber-attacks. It is therefore strategic for the state and organizations to adopt protection strategies and procedures, which is being done through the NIS directive. However, every company should reflect on how an attack on these infrastructures can affect its operations, providing an emergency plan.

Network security

With a perimeter that is now permeable and given the risk of incorrect behavior by internal staff, network security can no longer limit itself to blocking unwanted accesses from outside the network, but also be concerned with monitoring suspicious behavior and segmenting internal resources. network in a granular way, for example by providing access only to people who have legitimate reasons to use it and preventing the compromise of a resource from posing a risk to the rest of the network. Segmentation sometimes requires trade-offs between security and convenience (adding additional logins can slow down operations but is often necessary). Many attacks, particularly those carried out by organized structures, are targeted at the most vulnerable, albeit insignificant, resource of a network. After taking control of it, the attacker makes "lateral shifts" on the network to infect the other computers on the network up to the most critical systems. It can take months or even years for a company to realize that its systems have been breached. Months during which the attacker was able to acquire information and control services. Modern threat detection systems usually collect a lot of data. The more advanced ones are able to correlate information from numerous security devices, from firewalls to server logs, from email to PC antivirus, using them as "sensors" to detect anomalies. In this way, a lot of data is collected and a lot of false reports can be generated (false positives). The artificial intelligence algorithms are used that are able to catalog and prioritize alarms, with personnel specialized in threat assessment.

Cloud security

Moving enterprise workloads to the cloud brings new security challenges, such as:

- The transfer of information on heterogeneous platforms of which you do not have full control or knowledge;

- In some cases, some instances can be created and then "forgotten";

- Variable billing coupled with automatic provisioning can have unforeseen consequences on IT costs;

- Attacks on vendors, particularly PaaS and SaaS, can impact customer security.

Cloud providers are creating new security tools that help business users secure their data, but the bottom line is that a migration to the cloud cannot be the excuse to delegate data protection to the provider and avoid doing the necessary controls on cybersecurity.

Among the cloud-specific cyber security tools, the Cloud Access Security Broker (CASB) is emerging, tools installed in the company or also in the cloud that allow you to define security policies and controls which are then applied to all cloud services used.

Application security

Application security (AppSec), and in particular that of web applications, has increased in importance because it represents one of the most vulnerable points lately, but still few organizations are able to adequately mitigate the main application vulnerabilities, which are mapped by the Open Web Application Security Project in its Top 10. Application security begins with the use of secure programming practices, among which the most recent trends are DevSecOps, an interpretation of DevOps in which security is addressed from the very beginning of the project on both sides (development and operations). One of the problems with DevOps projects is that often the speed of execution and the business needs lead to neglect the security aspect, or consider it something to be carried out only in the final phase. Application security should then be verified through penetration testing practices.

Data security

As indicated at the beginning of the book, computer security can be based on three aspects of data protection:

- Confidentiality: the data must be accessible only to those who are entitled to know them, and not by others. In addition to checking the identity of people, this is achieved through the encryption of data stored or in transit on the network.

- Availability: when requested by authorized persons (or by the public in the case of open websites and services), the data must be effectively served in good time. A threat in this case are attacks that aim to saturate the resources of a server to prevent its operation (Denial of Service), against which there are effective network defenses. To protect against the loss of stored data, even following ransomware-type attacks, backup structures and policies are required.

- Integrity: the data must not be able to be deleted but not even modified by anyone who is not authorized to do so, neither when they are archived nor when they are exported externally. Again, encryption - and in particular the branch of digital signature - can ensure that the message has not been tampered with.

User identity management

If, as we have seen, authentication is no longer dependent on belonging to a network domain, but is specific to each resource and application, the user's identity must be as certain as possible - thanks to the use of multiple authentication factors - but also fast and usable. Single- sign-on systems and federated authentication platforms can ensure smooth operations and security.

Email security

From trojans to ransomware, to less technical but no fewer devastating attacks such as phishing (especially in its "targeted" variant, spear phishing) or scams with which people who pretend to be company managers push employees to do unwanted actions, there are many cyber threats that use email as an attack vehicle. Anti-spam and anti-phishing systems provide a first level of protection, but the inherent insecurity of the protocols used in email, combined with the scarce diffusion of systems that could improve its reliability such as DMARC, continue to ensure that the email is among the company's most vulnerable points. Recent email protection solutions use sandboxing to analyze the effects of an attachment on the system before delivering it to the recipient, and combine information contained in the meta-data to try to detect suspicious emails, including using artificial intelligence algorithms.

Internet of Things Security

The Internet of Thing worries security experts for the heterogeneity of the systems to be protected and for the scarce care towards cybersecurity that so far has been placed by the manufacturers of various types of devices, their short persistence on the market, and the scarce availability of security patches. Concerns addressed in particular to two perhaps opposing aspects. On the one hand, industrial control systems could be used to induce failures or create catastrophic accidents on plants and infrastructures. On the other hand, more anonymous and apparently harmless equipment can be used as a bridgehead to breach a network and subsequently lead to attacks on central systems (an American casino suffered a serious economic loss following an attack that had its point origin in the aquarium thermostat in the game room). Two additional risks are unauthorized access to cameras and microphones that can be used to intercept and monitor company personnel, or the risk that IoT devices are used to create botnets capable of attacking other IT infrastructures, as in the case of the Mirai botnet.

Mobile Security

Cell phones and tablets used in the company carry specific risks. They are often used for both business and personal purposes (if they are not directly owned by the employee), they can contain data exposed to the risk of theft or loss, they are linked to a subscription that can generate even important costs and are not generally perceived as one IT tool to protect and protect as much as the PC, neither by the user, nor often by the IT departments. Mobile Device Management (MDM) systems are essential and allow IT security to manage software updates and installations and define usage policies for fleets of portable devices on different operating systems.

CYBERSECURITY AND CYBERWAR

IN 2021

GLOBAL CYBERSECURITY COOPERATION

Cybercrime is scarier than drug trafficking:
70% of Americans are alarmed

For nine out of ten citizens, hacker attacks represent a greater danger even than money laundering. And for 87% the scenario will get worse

70% of North American consumers are concerned about the misuse of personal data provided to websites when banking or shopping online. And the vast majority now see cybercrime as a threat to their country. A situation that, among other things, is perceived as worsening: nine out of ten Americans think that cybercrime is "an important challenge for the entire security of the United States". Cybercrime is even considered a more important threat than drug trafficking or money laundering. What is also worrying is the criticism reserved to what has been done so far by the police, whose efforts to fight cybercrime have been judged not sufficient.

These are some of the key results that emerged from the IT Security Barometer, a survey carried out by Eset, a company specializing in cyber security solutions, which involved 3,500 adults in North America (2,500 in the United

States and a thousand in Canada). The study was devised by government policy makers to assess public attitudes towards cybercrime, cyber security and data privacy and relies on a series of questions consistent with investigations conducted for the Commission in the countries of the Old Continent. The intent is to produce data that can be used by governments without there being any doubts about their neutrality.

Among the most alarming evidence of this survey is the lack of confidence that the situation will improve in the short term. About 87% of those involved said they expected an increased risk of becoming a victim of cybercrime. There are even those who think of reducing their online purchases or using home banking services (19% and 20% respectively) due to growing security and privacy problems, while 44% of respondents said that the problems with security and privacy have prompted them to provide less personal information on websites. However, while a very large number of people fear they could be victims of identity theft (86%), the percentage of respondents who reported having suffered an identity theft was much less than half (30%)

G7, the key factor cooperation to strengthen cyber security

In addition to the document on SMEs and that on artificial intelligence, the ministers of ICT and industry of the seven powers, meeting in the G7, agreed on a statement on the subject of cyber security.

The actions of the G7 to improve the cyber security of companies

Objective 1 - Development and implementation of an appropriate management of cyber security risks

The wider use of ICT technologies carries the risk of an increase in the number of cyber incidents and breaches that can cause severe disruption in modern society and severe economic damage to businesses. Furthermore, such incidents can also undermine citizens 'and businesses' confidence in the digital society and discourage the use of digital technologies. Poor risk management can threaten all partners within value chains and production networks, with consequent effects on national and regional economies. For this reason, ways need to be explored to raise awareness, especially SMEs, of cyber risks and encourage the adoption of good consumer practices.

To this end, the G7 ICT and Industry Ministers intend to:

- encourage businesses, especially SMEs, at top management level, to raise awareness and adopt effective cyber security;

- promote cooperation between governments and businesses, particularly SMEs, by involving industry associations, academia, technology community associations, security researchers and the cyber risk insurance industry, in order to improve the database on the economic and commercial repercussions of cyber security and data breach incidents;

Objective 2 - Improve cooperation

Cooperation is the key factor in strengthening cybersecurity. Between technical-operational bodies, between governments and between governments and businesses.

Effective and constructive cooperation between G7 countries, national CSIRTs (cyber security intervention groups) and between CSIRTs and businesses can increase the chances of preventing and responding to cyber threats through reliable and trusted channels for exchanging information and action information about potential and emerging threats. In this context, the role of national CSIRTs is important as the main focal point, in particular for information sharing at the technical and operational level. Assessing business exposure to cyber security threats and developing appropriate internal practices can help businesses, especially SMEs, improve the security and resilience of their business processes.

Lack of knowledge makes enterprises vulnerable to cyber threats and attacks. The G7 countries should seek to increase the culture of cyber security and to raise awareness of cyber security, especially among companies.

The protection of critical information infrastructure (CIIP) is part of the digital agenda of many countries and international organizations. Some countries have already established a national framework and are reviewing their guidelines on this. For this reason, we G7 ICT and Industry

CYBERSECURITY AND CYBERWAR IN 2021

Ministers intend to explore new ways to enhance cooperation between the public and private sectors.

To this end we mean:

- promote constructive cooperation between the national CSIRTs of the G7 countries and between CSIRTs and businesses of all sizes, in order to foster an exchange of information on cyber threats and vulnerabilities;

- examine common ways to assess the exposure of companies to cyber security threats and to assess the effectiveness of the corresponding cyber security measures

- Governments and civil society to consider a range of different approaches, such as security-by-design, good risk management practices, market relevant compliance assessments and process appropriate security assessments, to improve security throughout the value chain and promote greater confidence in the digital economy.

- conducting awareness campaigns among SMEs about cyber security risks and how to manage them;

- support initiatives aimed at promoting a culture of cooperation, particularly between governments and businesses, for a more effective knowledge of cyber threats

- promote the exchange of information through the collaboration of operators of critical computerized infrastructures such as ISACs (Information sharing and analysis centers) or its equivalent.

- promote global dialogue for cooperation and sharing of good practices among all stakeholders, including cyber security risk management, in order to foster economic prosperity.

Trump is looking for 300,000 operators to bridge the cyber gap in the US

The president signed an executive order: "This is an incredible economic opportunity for American workers." Among the initiatives is the organization of a cyber competition called "President's Cup".

To defend the ever-wider perimeter of digital spaces, there is a need for cutting-edge technological barriers, but also the skills necessary to develop, activate and maintain them. The so-called 'skill gap' in cyber security - the shortage of adequately qualified personnel in the sector - is a global issue, which the United States will now try to address thanks to the provisions contained in an executive order signed in recent hours by President Donald Trump.

THE OBJECTIVES

Because of the growing number of cyber-attacks that just in 2018, according to the FBI, cost American companies the enormous sum of three billion dollars and a lack of professionals, especially on the public side, the main objectives pursued by the White House with the measures are to increase the workforce in the field of information security within the federal government (also thanks to the resources provided in the new budget), to improve mobility in an extremely sensitive sector, as well as to support the development of skills by encouraging training of new excellence. But it is not just a technical initiative. True to his intentions to push the accelerator of the economy, the president commented that the professions surrounding the cybersecurity area "represent an incredible economic opportunity for American workers," particularly at such a delicate time as the years of the race for technology. "These actions," Trump stressed closely followed by National Security Advisor John Bolton, "will allow more Americans to get (well-paid) jobs that increase our nation's wealth and increase our security."

THE NUMBERS OF THE SKILL GAP

Currently, about 300,000 cybersecurity operators are needed in the United States alone. A number that, according to what is written in the document, needs to be reversed to guarantee Washington the maintenance of the current competitive advantage at international level in the field of cyber security (as well as a high level of defense to stem the dangers posed by those who are considered from the United States the main threats to American national security, in particular the so-called 'cyber axis' made up of China, North Korea, Iran and Russia).

NEW FOR DHS

To achieve these goals, the executive order states that the Department of Homeland Security - responsible for the protection of national critical infrastructures and led ad interim by Kevin McAleenan , (after the exit of cyber expert Kirstjen Nielsen) - will collaborate with partners from across the government on a series of initiatives to boost cyber workforce numbers. In particular, Homeland Security will have to create a professional rotation program, in which IT (Information Technology) and cyber security professionals within the federal government can carry out temporary assignments in the DHS and vice versa. This initiative should enable the sharing of cybersecurity best practices (including training courses) and provide an exchange of valuable experiences for the workforce. Furthermore, Homeland Security will have the burden of carrying out aptitude assessments to understand who might be considered a valid candidate to work in the sector.

THE OTHER OFFICES

Together with the Department of Defense, the White House Office of Science and Technology, the Office of Management and Budgeting and other partner agencies, the DHS will plan a cyber competition called the "President's Cup". The initiative will serve to stimulate competition and incentivize military, professionals and anyone with a level of expertise in the field of cyber security. In summary, the executive order attempts to strengthen collaboration between the various departments in a sector that requires continuous updating of skills. The importance of intervening on the security of critical infrastructures is then highlighted, especially as regards the identification of vulnerabilities and gaps in the skills of employees. Moreover, thanks to the provision, training courses have also been encouraged, in particular for the defense sector.

The advent, after the four traditional dimensions (land, air, sea and outer space), of a fifth dimension of conflict linked to the cyber element has imposed an original effort by nation states to update their respective national security doctrines. The dual-use nature of information technologies, easily reused for military purposes, the lowering of the threshold for access to IT tools determined by the diffusion of low-cost hardware and digital democratization processes, as well as the intrinsic trade-off, or inversely proportional relationship, between computerization and security that characterizes densely computerized companies, in fact determine the birth of new threats to national security on a cyber level; threats that change and progress with the same speed of technological innovation and that therefore oblige the legislator to offer a flexible, careful and versatile response.

In this regard, in May 2017 the Presidency of the Council of Ministers released the new National Plan for Cyber Protection and Information Security, conceived to identify "the operational guidelines, the objectives to be achieved and the lines of action to be implemented to the National Framework for the security of the cyber space (QSN), in light of the guidelines for cyber protection and information security indicated by the President of the Council of Ministers in their capacity as the top body of the national cyber architecture ".

The strategic guidelines of the National Strategic Framework (QSN), prepared by the Cyber Technical Table (TTC) - which operates at the DIS and in which the cyber representatives of the CISR (Foreign Affairs, Interior, Defense, Justice, Economy and Finance, Economic Development) participate), the Digital Agency and the Cyber Security Nucleus (NSC) - are the following:

- Strengthening the defense capabilities of national Critical Infrastructures and of the actors of strategic importance for the country system;

- Improvement, according to an integrated approach, of the technological, operational and analytical skills of the institutional actors involved;

- Encouragement of cooperation between national institutions and companies;

- Promotion and dissemination of the culture of cyber security;

- Strengthening international cooperation on cyber security;

- Strengthening of abilities to combat illegal activities and online content.

CYBERSECURITY AND CYBERWAR IN 2021

To give substance to the strategic guidelines of the QSN, the National Plan (NP) has identified 11 operational guidelines, of which we report the foundations.

- Strengthening of intelligence, police and civil and military defense capabilities. "National cyber protection and cyber security, in order to be effectively pursued, presupposes, in the first instance, an in-depth knowledge of vulnerabilities - not only of the technological factor but also of the human one - and of the cyber threats that exploit them, in order to making networks and systems, especially in the case of critical infrastructures, more resilient, while at the same time ensuring the effectiveness of the contrast ".

- Strengthening the organization and coordination and interaction methods at national level between public and private entities. "This policy aims to strengthen coordination and cooperation not only between the various public entities, but also between these and private entities, considering that the latter manage national critical infrastructures. Hence the need to ensure interoperability between the various players, even at an international level".

- Promotion and dissemination of the culture of information security. "Up to now, education and training in the IT security sector has been mainly aimed at specialized personnel who work or who are destined to operate in the sector. Therefore, the need arises for an activity to promote the culture of information security aimed at a wide public, which includes private citizens and staff, and businesses ".

- International cooperation and exercises. "The transnational nature of the cyber threat and its pervasiveness require an international approach to the issue, given that individual states must necessarily act synergistically to deal with it. This necessarily presupposes a common level of preparation and interoperability".

- Operation of the national incident prevention, response and remediation structures. "The preparation of prevention and reaction capacities to cyber events requires the development of Computer Emergency Team (CERT) as providers of technical assistance, research and development, training and information services for their respective public and / or private users. The NIS Directive provides, at least in favor of essential service managers, a new type of organization intended as an evolution of CERTs capable of ensuring effective assistance and active support capacity constituent in the event of a cybernetic event. In the context of the implementation of the innovations introduced by the NIS Directive, it is necessary to redefine the role played by the actors present in the current national architecture (the various CERTs) and those who will enter it (in addition to CSIRT, National Authority/s and single point of contact). Pending the transposition of the NIS directive, a process of progressive unification of public CERTs will be launched to establish, in the sectors of strategic interest, the exclusive competence of a single national CERT, or to create a national network of CERTs by identifying a subject with powers of coordination ".

- Legislative interventions and compliance with international obligations. "The rapid technological-information evolution entails an equally rapid obsolescence of the rules governing matters related to information and communication technologies. Therefore, they require periodic reviews and updates, as well as additions, also to create a legal substrate for the activities carried out for the purposes of cyber protection and IT security and to make administrators and users responsible for the operations they perform on the systems assigned to them. ".

- Compliance with standards and security protocols. "Compliance with security standards and protocols, developed both nationally and internationally, allows us to guarantee a common and high level of quality in ensuring cyber protection and IT security of systems and networks".

- Support for industrial and technological development. "The guarantee of the reliability and safety of hardware and software components produced in the USA and other countries, especially those used by critical infrastructures and by subjects that carry out activities of strategic importance for the country, represents an objective that can be achieved only if all actors in the value chain (hardware component manufacturers, software developers , information society service providers) will make security a priority ".

- Strategic communication. "The communication about a cyber event and its consequences assumes strategic importance, since the individual Administrations concerned and the private entities managing essential services must be able to provide, where necessary or appropriate, complete, correct information, truthful and transparent, without thereby creating unnecessary alarmism that would amplify the economic and social impact of the event itself ".

"The starting point for careful financial planning and for the allocation of resources is the analysis of the costs of occurring or potential cyber events, since the importance of the risk is directly proportional to the probability and extent of the damage. Likewise, the opportunity and priority of intervention on a specific vulnerability could be better supported at the decision-making level if accompanied by the appropriate elements of economic evaluation."

Implementation of a Cyber Risk Management system "The protection of data from threats that affect its authenticity, integrity, confidentiality and availability is an integral part of this National Plan as the information constitutes an intrinsic value of the organization, public or private, and the essential objective of every cyber-attack ".

On 24 June 2018, following the NIS (Network and Information Security) directive of July 2016, aimed at addressing the cyber issue by increasing the level of cyber security in the 28 member countries, the legislative decree of implementation came into force, which in addition to dealing with issues already framed by the National Plan (NP), such as promoting the culture of security, limiting the impact of cyber incidents and strengthening cooperation at national level, establishes new "obligations in the field of security and notification for so-called Essential Service Operators (OSE) - i.e. public or private organizations operating in the energy, transport, banking, financial market infrastructure, digital infrastructure, health and drinking water supply and distribution sectors - and for Digital Service Providers (FSD): e-commerce, search engines, and cloud computing".

There are three points on which it is good to pause to highlight the positive work carried out by the Cyber Technical Table (TTC) and by the bodies that have dealt with processing the various assets of today's cybernetic architecture of the country:

- `The concept of cyber protection and information security not as a goal, but as a "process". The fluid, adaptive and changing reality of cyberspace requires the constitution of flexible, modular and dynamic defensive structures, which consider cyber security not as a static goal, but as an uninterrupted succession of new arrival and departure lines. Technological innovation involves transformations with a significant impact on an almost daily basis and the growing computational power of modern processors will imply in the short term an even more marked increase in the offensive potential offered by the cyber dimension, moreover at decreasing costs. Considering IT security as a "process", albeit obvious, denotes special attention to these aspects and can only be appreciated.

- Overall rationalization of the country's cyber architecture and contraction of the chain of command and control. The ordinary and extraordinary management of national cyber security is attributed to the structures of the DIS (Department of Information for Security), the NISP is abolished and the Cyber Security Nucleus (NSC), is repositioned at the DIS. Furthermore, the chain of command responsible for crisis management will undergo an overall process of contraction, "in order to make the action of the bodies called to carry out response and remediation tasks in the event of cyber events prompt and effective ". The two CERTs, then reunited in the CSIRT must interact closely to allow an operational alignment that ensures "a unitary capacity for detection, alarm and first analysis of cyber incidents". In a nutshell, all the segments of society interested in the cyber issue are incorporated in a unitary system orbiting around the DIS. This choice, in a context of digital balkanization without driving forces and stable anchoring points, can certainly be considered a good choice, especially if combined with the desire to create, in the cyber environment, a real institutional network that operates in unison. for a common purpose, which in the main case is national security. The constitution of a reticular cybernetic architecture allows a more careful control by the institutional bodies responsible for monitoring cybernetic events and a significantly greater capacity to react, in compliance with the principle of "concentration of forces" of Clausewitzian memory.

- Empowerment of all actors involved in various capacities in the issue. The establishment of a network of actors, public and private, who cooperate and collaborate in order to consolidate the national security of the country originates from the empowerment of the same, a process that leads them to consider themselves not as separate units, but as part of a system. Connecting all the nodes of the network, in a world that has made the network its main architrave, is the only way to create a truly effective defensive complex.

If these three principles, i.e. the perception of cyber security as a process, the concentration of forces through organizational centralization and the empowerment of all the actors involved, remain firm and central to the government agenda, the cyber architecture of the country system can hope to reach an even greater threshold of effectiveness, keep up with the evolution of the situation on a global scale, withstand the confrontation with the dynamism of technological innovation, and therefore raise a stable and resilient defensive bastion in the fifth dimension of conflict.

THE NEW CRIMINAL SCENARIOS

The relentless development of information technology in recent decades has brought about epochal changes in every area of human life. This technology offers multiple opportunities for development on a social, cultural and economic level, but also represents a fertile ground for new methods of aggression against legal assets, having a criminal relevance, and, therefore, a new frontier in the fight against crime, which can offer innovative tools and means for finding evidence and, in general, for combating serious criminal phenomena.

The counterpart to the physiology of Information and Communication Technology is constituted by the pathology of cybercrime, understood as the complex of actions with criminal purposes, which are perpetuated in cyberspace (think of computer fraud, identity theft, extortion from ransomware, to online recycling, etc.).

Cybercrime can therefore be considered a phenomenon that represents the result of the evolution of information technology, which, like any technological innovation, has brought with it security problems, which, in the context of technologies, are identified as ontological problems, as they are inherent in the very nature of technology.

The transnationality of criminal phenomena, also having a cyber nature, represents a great challenge for States, for the evolution of criminal policies, and entails the need to give impetus to a new ideological and methodological approach of global scope. This need is felt more in the context of computer crimes, since moving from a tangible and material environment to an intangible and dematerialized environment means that the offenses committed and the tools and methods used to investigate them are no longer subject to traditional and pre-established rules.

In this regard, the rules governing traditional means of communication are today, in the face of the new virtual domain coinciding with the cyber space, inadequate, if not obsolete, as they are built with reference to a physical and territorial space. In such a context, it is clearly difficult to extend them to include the actions carried out in the cybernetic environment, since this is of a delocalized and territorial nature.

Until now, every criminal organization, even those capable of branching out on an extraterritorial level, was born from and within a specific territory. These organizations identified themselves with their territory of origin, on which they were rooted with their cultural codes, with their traditions. These organizations were characterized by a close bond and direct knowledge between the members. Cybercrime, on the other hand, is distinguished, for example, by the transnational connotation of the crime, which is borderless, i.e. without borders or a-spatial, an unprecedented feature among all crimes, which is unprecedented in history in traditional criminal activities and which makes it the crime par excellence of the third millennium.

Add to this, as a distinctive feature of the criminal threat in cyberspace, the distance between cybercriminals and their potential victims. Illicit cyber conduct can take the form of multiple actions, carried out at different times or simultaneously by multiple agents or by just one in a multiplicity of places or in a virtual space. The aforementioned conduct engages several processing and information transfer processes, which pass in a long time or in real time through indeterminate spaces. One or more victims can be affected by the cyber-attack, immediately or after some time.

Given the characteristics of the cybercriminal threat, it is clear that the cybercriminal is in a position of advantage over the traditional criminal.

Information Age: orienting yourself in the new era

Today's era corresponds to the Information Age, because each individual has the right to freely transfer information and can have immediate access to that knowledge, which previously, at best, he would have found with difficulty.

We have therefore arrived at a system of "open communication", which eliminates any kind of demarcation between "protected information" and "wide-open information". The man of the third millennium therefore has the urgent need to be able to count on the continuous use of data and information, as if to demonstrate and justify his very existence.

The development of digital technologies, aimed at functions such as the production, processing, dissemination, transmission and use of information, has undoubtedly led to an acceleration of the daily life and lifestyle of the individual, favoring communications, fast connections and global, which are shaping modern society, making it digital.

CYBERSECURITY AND CYBERWAR
IN 2021

The aforementioned technologies have defined new and greater opportunities on a planetary scale, thus resulting in a better quality of life for ever larger sections of the population.

In a very short space of time, most human activities, performed manually or through mechanical equipment, have given way too much more efficient digital implementations. In the context of commercial and relationship life, legal acts and transactions of various kinds are regulated and executed through orders, given to electronic processors, which modify legal spheres and carry out transfers of capital in an intangible form.

The evolutionary process, determined by the advent of sophisticated processing and communication technologies, has not only entailed changes in the nature of information, but has led to substantial changes in its dissemination. In the first place, the amplitude has varied: the information has progressively reached at the same time an increasing number of subjects even hundreds of thousands of kilometers away from each other. Secondly, the speed has changed radically, becoming hyperbolic: the information, once subsequent to the facts to which it referred, became first immediately consequent, then even simultaneous.

Information and Communications Technologies (ICT) are now pervasive and are penetrating transversally into all production sectors and systems that regulate social dynamics: public services, knowledge, media convergence, social networks, environmental management, energy problems, agriculture and the working world. Organized companies, therefore, are evolving towards an interaction model enabled by ICT anytime, anywhere, for anybody.

It is necessary to relate to the size of the internet population to better understand this highly digitized scenario.

According to the Global Digital 2018 report by We Are Social, out of 7.6 billion inhabitants on the planet, Internet users are 4 billion (53% of the world population), and of these, 3.2 billion (42%) are active on social media. This data can allow us to understand how great the criminal impact on the so-called Internet galaxy can be.

In particular, for young people the exposure to digital far exceeds that of school attendance and, even, that dedicated to night rest, so the media can be transformed into "weapons of mass distraction", with evident repercussions on preparation school, on social relationships and also on the psyche.

Ultimately it may be noted that the Information Age presents great opportunities for humanity as a whole, but that it has also paved the way for risks, threats of all kinds, difficult to predict events and conflicts between individual, collective, state or safety.

The information revolution and its problematic profiles

CYBERSECURITY AND CYBERWAR IN 2021

Fruition, influence and innovation are the three key concepts of the information revolution, which society has been experiencing globally since 1995 and shows no sign of dying out.

This, determined by the transition from industrial society to the information or information society, has led to a succession of profound consequences, not only on the national and supranational regulatory heritage, but also on social and political relationships, on the type and quality of interpersonal relationships, on leisure, on the distribution of knowledge, on education, on commerce, on health, on the language used within the social body and so on. In such a context, the IT tools affect the arrangement of the activities just mentioned, conforming them to algorithmic and digital structures, without distorting their essence but modifying their form.

This passage has influenced social paradigms, introducing, according to the sociologist Castells, a new socio-technological paradigm, characterized by some aspects: the raw material of the new technologies is information; the effects of new technologies possess a great pervasiveness; new technologies allow and encourage interconnection between technological systems, are flexible and tend towards convergence.

This revolution, however, is very difficult to control, since it has suddenly made the average man the master of a new and immense universe, for which the institutions no longer assume an undisputed dominant position, finding themselves instead on par, if not at times at a disadvantage, compared to the indeterminate number of subjects involved.

Although the advantages and benefits brought by the so-called "cyber tsunami" are truly manifold, to the point that today it would be impossible to think of living in an unconnected world, the Internet is still an indeterminate, open, decentralized and neutral universe.

Technological advancement has made means available to a multitude of subjects, which enormously expand the range of human potential, but without the necessary adjustments to the ethical and regulatory framework. In the context that has emerged, the exponential growth of information technologies, not balanced by adequate legal regulation, has generated a gray space, where it is possible to act with impunity for antisocial purposes, ranging from cybercrime to cyberwar.

The national and international rules governing traditional means of communication (radio, press, television, publishing) are, in the face of the new dimension of the cyber space, profoundly inadequate, as they have been devised thinking of a territorial space and, clearly, it is complex to extend them to include also the operations carried out through the Network since the latter creates a virtual space consisting of websites and web pages, which are not located in a specific physical place. The law-cyberspace relationship therefore produces a series of relevant problematic profiles, including those relating to the identification of the criminal action and the location of the perpetrator of the cyber-crime.

CYBERSECURITY AND CYBERWAR IN 2021

The incessant evolution, but also the new demands of globalization, as well as the birth of new legal goods, hitherto unknown, with the consequent new threats to them constitute factors of rapid aging of the rules and pose to the jurist the problem of a constant search for rules, new ones that better balance different interests.

The digital evolution should therefore be matched by an ethical-normative evolution, capable of making the 2.0 revolution usable in safety. The cyber-individual must consciously take on the task of controlling technological progress, directing him towards a desired improvement of his own and others' living conditions, providing a regulatory framework suitable for the purpose. And this is not an easy task, as it involves a conscious control of the technology in question and its evolutions.

Cyberspace: the fifth dimension of conflict

The concept of cyberspace deserves some more in-depth consideration: the technological substrate where one of the new manifestations of today's crime is perpetuated, as well as a crucial element for the political, social, financial and human dynamics of the 21st century.

It can well be said, in fact, that today daily life flows on thousands and thousands of kilometers of cables and optical fibers that connect the most remote nodes of the globe in a very intricate, dense and capillary network. Data, information, images and economic provisions run lightning fast in the intangible, immaterial and timeless dimension of cyber space: a sort of "non-place", in which the entire social, economic, political and military system of the whole moves and feeds planet.

This term, apparently futuristic, contains in reality in a succinct but effective way a new and complex universe, fascinating and dangerous, virtual and at the same time dramatically concrete, on which much of the vitality of the modern world flows.

This new "space" dimension presents itself, by its very nature, as "deterritorialized", "decentralized" and characterized by simultaneity, anonymity, "depersonalization" and " detemporalization " of activities.

Before focusing on the characteristics of cyberspace we must, first of all, give a definition. This is a task that is not easy to complete, due to the particular nature that connotes it.

The "peculiarity" of cyberspace, in fact, is essentially due to the competition in its formulation of both natural and virtual elements, whose "hybrid" nature reflects the uncertainty and inability to reach an all-encompassing sharing of the cognitive description of the term in question.

For the purposes of our discussion, however, we can, here, refer to the "National Strategic Framework for the Security of the Cyber Space" which defines the cyber space as "the set of interconnected IT infrastructures, including hardware, software, data and users, as well as the logical relationships, however established, between them. It therefore includes the Internet, communication networks, the systems on which the computerized data processing processes are based and mobile devices equipped with a network connection. [...] "It constitutes a virtual domain of strategic importance for the economic, social and cultural development of nations ".

Defined as the "fifth dimension of conflict", cyber space lends itself to being the new battleground and geopolitical competition in the 21st century; artificial theater of war supplementary to the four natural theaters of land, sea, air and extra-atmospheric space; a fascinating domain, which represents one of the most critical fields of international politics today and potentially tomorrow, as well as a concrete threat to national and international security.

Cyber space, a virtual environment and the par excellence of human activity, presents itself differently from the four traditional domains. More than an additional dimension, it is identified as an environment, which envelops the other areas of human action. In fact, given the pervasiveness that characterizes it, it penetrates transversally into all production sectors and into the systems that regulate social dynamics: public services, knowledge, social networks, environmental management, air, maritime and railway traffic control, management of domestic appliances or personal medical devices and business world.

CYBERSECURITY AND CYBERWAR
IN 2021

A dimension full of unknowns, but not entirely obscure. There are, in fact, some considerations that can be made regarding the characteristics of this new cyberworld:

- It is constantly evolving: the pervasiveness of the Internet goes hand in hand with the development of IT infrastructures and with the expansion of political, commercial and economic relations between States;

- Alongside the four traditional domains, cyberspace can be used as a strategic tool by states. Cybernetic power can be used, in fact, in peace and in war; it's hidden, relatively cheap, and allows for both offense and defense. It also guarantees results as effective as those of conventional military tools, but at a fraction of the cost;

- Cyberspace is the latest evolution of a technological journey that began centuries ago. The printing press, telegraph, telephone and wireless communication technologies have also revolutionized societies and economies. Unlike all its predecessors, cyber space is not just a communication tool but a means of creating, accumulating, manipulating and destroying information.

- Cyber space is terra nullius. It is precisely the absence of rules that makes it attractive to pursue criminal or aggressive purposes in political, economic, social and religious terms. Furthermore, it was not designed or engineered to be a safe place but, on the contrary, to convey information. This results in an intrinsic security deficit, which makes it a persistent offensive environment.

CYBERSECURITY AND CYBERWAR IN 2021

- Cyberspace is, in the final analysis, an ocean of information, which has no defined borders, but only "spaces" with particularly mobile ends; a new perspective, devoid of any reference and characterized by instant and globalized information.

Problematic profiles of cyber space

Cyberspace is the new geopolitical battlefield and competition of the 21st century. This new dimension has the (unique) capacity to make political imbalances, which dominate international relations, uniform, placing subjects of the most diverse nature on the chessboard: single individuals, non-state actors and states. These act on an almost equal playing field, thus eliminating any form of asymmetry. In every act of war, in fact, the physicality of those who act on land, sea, air or space makes the actors easily identifiable, just as the borders of the belligerent state are also easily identifiable.

The same does not happen in cyber space, where, due to its intrinsic digitized nature, it is very complex not only to attribute the action in a timely manner to one or more specific subjects and / or to a State, but also to understand the reason for the attack and its objectives. Above all, those who have acted can easily escape from any legal, political, diplomatic, economic and military responsibility.

The aforementioned "space", if on the one hand it contains within itself the potential to allow an

CYBERSECURITY AND CYBERWAR IN 2021

unprecedented development of the economic and productive activities of commerce, of the efficiency of public administrations and the exercise of people's rights in unprecedented forms, on the other it constitutes the occasion for the new forms of threat to productive activities, to the enjoyment of citizens' freedoms, to the action of public powers and of the States themselves. The threat, although referring to the intangible world of cyber space, presents itself with features of extreme concreteness and is assuming an ever-greater importance in the concerns of governments.

The cyber space is, moreover, a terrain of action similar to the mythical "Wild West", in which lawmen and criminals confront each other. If the absence of physical barriers makes cyber space the ideal terrain in which to "throw the stone", anonymity, guaranteed by the Net, also makes it the perfect context in which to "hide the hand".

Ultimately, the security of cyber space has reached a strategic connotation that is absolutely comparable to that of the protection of physical space, so much so that it represents one of the major concerns and sources of investment by the main world players, considering that the Internet is now understood as the critical infrastructure par excellence. States cannot, therefore, ignore what happens in cyberspace and, on the contrary, must equip themselves, even in this new dimension, with tools to protect against attacks that can cause damage or prejudice to the free and orderly development of human activities and exercise primary citizenship rights. Ultimately, States are now called upon to devise, plan and implement defense measures, just as they have always done to defend real spaces.

From the digital revolution to the criminal revolution

It would be superficial to overlook the potential dark side of the information revolution that is taking place. Like any technology, having no intrinsic moral connotation, it can be used for both good and evil.

The process of computerized neovascularization and the new frontiers of communication, opened by the Net, have already affected every sector of human activity for some time, becoming an omnipresent aspect in the daily life of work and private environments. In this broad trail, the effect of potential expansion of illicit activities and the expansion of the diffusive capacity of criminal behavior is inevitable. The spread of these two realities, just mentioned, has determined the exponential increase in information, created, communicated and stored in digital form. Computers and electronic equipment thus become, with increasing frequency, protagonists and faithful witnesses of the crime.

If it is true that crime has accompanied humanity since the dawn of its evolutionary history, adapting in form as in content to the changing social reality, then, in this sense, the digital revolution has also represented a sort of criminal revolution: after the first moments of uncertainty, information technologies have confirmed their fertile ground, in which the new expressions of organized crime occupy an ever greater space, directly proportional to the computerization process that is underway.

The speed of the Internet, capable of moving large masses of information from one part of the world to another in fractions of a second, has been recognized as a winning weapon by criminal organizations, which have not been slow to use electronic highways to run their own money, coming from the most disparate illicit operations. It is vital for criminal organizations to ensure a flow of financial resources, which must subsequently be reinvested. These resources are functional to the corruption of public officials. In such a context, the Internet lends itself well to these purposes, both allowing the perpetration of computer fraud and promoting online money laundering, so-called cyberlaundering, and facilitating the exchange of information, avoiding dangerous communication dynamics, represented by direct contact.

In the so-called "all-encompassing" technology society, organized crime is conforming to the digital revolution, the continuous expansion of electronic commerce, the increasingly incentivized spread of online banking services and the widespread use of electronic payments instruments. If, therefore, all the interests and propositive activities of the company move to the Net, consequently, also the set of illicit conduct will follow its evolution in forms and practices.

Therefore, technological progress has been accompanied by a constant and unstoppable growth of the activities carried out by cyber criminals, whose goal is no longer notoriety, but the implementation of a real business model different from the past, as it is organized, as stable as possible and able to survive over time. Today we are, in fact, in the presence of real criminal organizations, managed by subjects motivated by important and lasting profits, deriving, for example from the sale of personal data and cloned credit cards or from cyber-extortion by ransomware.

With Web 2.0, the creation, diffusion and use of malware cease to be artisanal operations, which act in an "informal" manner. A real division of duties and work develops, transforming the world of virus writers into the advanced tertiary sector of organized cybercrime.

Moreover, the division of labor of computer experts, who study vulnerabilities in operating systems and software, and rather than disclose their results to the developers of software in question, write exploits, online selling them in appropriate forums.

Against the backdrop of this new criminal landscape, characters from the anthology of Italian crime and terrorism can, with good reason, be replaced in the collective imagination by enterprising IT connoisseurs, refined minds and mere criminal workers, who present themselves with the same ambitions and determination to commit a crime as their predecessors.

This consideration does not differ so much from what was found by the former National Anti-Mafia Prosecutor Pietro Grasso, according to whom "classic" crime is changing the approach to new technologies, also thanks to the new generations, passing more and more often from "paper" to "telematic" ones, entrusting their secrets to the "hellish" and almost magical machines of the computer world, to the point of even living hiding on Facebook".

The phenomenon of cybercrime

The capillary expansion of the so-called seventh continent, coinciding with the Internet, has focused the attention of criminals towards new forms of crimes, allowing to design a new criminal scenario, cybercrime, a criminal phenomenon, in which the commission of the criminally relevant computer crime takes place in cyberspace through the use of information or telematic technologies.

From the traditional forms of expression of crime, aimed at drawing on values intrinsically attributable to the person (such as, for example, physical integrity or the patrimonial sphere), the concept of cybercrime, as a phenomenon in which information technology assumes, in itself, a leading role in the legal system both as an objective of the unlawful action, legally recognized and protected, and as a means of consummation of the crime, at the same time qualified and qualifying with respect to specific cases.

The complexity of the scenario and the intrinsically anonymous nature of the Network do not allow an easy attribution of specific legal responsibilities. Above all, criminals have taken advantage of this situation, who, to carry out certain actions, can be found anywhere in the world and from there they are able to act undisturbed. In addition, in order to carry out their illegal operations on the Net, they can interpose a variable number of intermediaries between the victim and the criminal, so as to make the detection of the offense and the attribution of responsibility difficult and complex. Moreover, most of the time, such brokers are unaware of their role within the crime network.

Cybercrime has taken on the contours of a real underground economy (a phenomenon that includes not only illegal activities, but also undeclared income, deriving from the production and sale of goods and services and monetary transactions and all legal economic activities, but not declared, to which the tax authorities could apply a taxable amount), globalized and efficient, where illegally stolen goods and fraudulent services are sold and purchased and where the estimated turnover is measurable in millions of dollars.

CYBERCRIME AS A NEW FACE OF ORGANIZED CRIME

The difficult issue of cybercrime has undergone heavy and decisive evolutions in the last twenty years, to the point of transforming itself from a topic to a serious problem.

Cybercrime is nothing more than the natural evolution of crime towards new illegal actions: if it is true that every new technology opens the doors to new types of criminal actions, it is evident that the application of modern information and telematic technologies to declared illegal actions is to all intents and purposes inevitable. With the development of information technologies, therefore, there has been a digitization of organized crime.

To give some examples, think of the invention of the automobile at the beginning of the century. It was obviously a new technology, which made it possible to travel with a limited number of passengers from one end of the country to the other. But this had a reflex effect: the car thieves made their appearance. Subsequently, the obligation of the plates was introduced, to allow easier identification of stolen vehicles; as a result, thieves began stealing license plates and forging them.

In the same way, the introduction of the mobile phone, almost a hundred years later, allowed, in fact, the birth of the so-called snatch and run, that is the theft of the mobile phone on the street, while the owner is using it. The subsequent explosion of the mobile communications market, in large mass distribution, has led to the birth of phenomena such as cyberstalking. Think also of digital cameras and video cameras, exploited by child pornography, electronic banking services and online sales, which offer fertile ground for computer fraud.

It is therefore normal, if not inevitable, that each technology opens the way to new criminal actions.

Crime is continually looking for uncontrolled places to conduct their criminal business with confidence. The Network undoubtedly represents a "free zone", as it can provide sufficient guarantees of security and anonymity. The spatial multidimensionality of this is in fact perfectly suited to this model of activity and to the effort to raise illicit profits within an acceptable degree of risk.

The transnational dimension of cybercrime

The globalization of information, generated by the advent of new technologies, has allowed the creation of a free market without borders, in which cybercrime takes on transnational backgrounds and reflections and proliferates at the speed of data exchange on the Internet, under the catalytic effect of it's difficulty to control, exercisable on the traffic of information, transiting on the Internet.

Cybercrime has therefore become globalized. In this regard, a relevant problem in the international community must be taken into consideration, coinciding with the relationship between the globalization process and the phenomenon of transnational crime.

If, in fact, the globalization process, on the one hand, has contributed to enhancing the opportunities for activities worthy of protection, on the other hand it has facilitated the development and sophistication of criminal groups, which operate on transnational markets. The numerous opportunities created by globalization, such as the abolition of borders, the creation of new business, new markets and the provision of new, more powerful and sophisticated means of communication and exchange, have been fully exploited by criminal groups, representing the ideal preconditions. for carrying out large-scale criminal activities.

Therefore, we are witnessing the birth of a new crime, which escapes traditional models and which aspires to control global economic trafficking, allocating part of the lucrative proceeds of this activity to the financing of further illicit trafficking, in a growing and negative spiral for the contemporary economy.

The new modern economy of globalization and the Internet is essentially based on five pillars of crime: financial transactions, which represent the recycling of all other forms of crime, the trade in arms and toxic-harmful materials, the trade in living organs dissected for transplants, the trade in natural and synthetic drugs, the pollution and plundering of the environment and cybercrime. All the forms of crime listed have a single glue that unifies and merges them with the circuits of the economy: finance.

Thus, transnational crime represents a serious threat to the economic and financial systems of all States, especially as a result of the current inability of contemporary society to deal with new criminal phenomena, due not so much to new forms of crime, but more to ineffectiveness. of the remedies proposed by some parties.

The Net, understood as a means of communication symbol of globalization, represents in itself something immediately perceptible by all as transnational. It is a transnationality, so to speak, for computer crimes, or at least, for those relating to the use of computer or telematic means as such, such as the use of IT systems and the internet for the cross-border transfer of data (think of cyberterrorism, the illicit use of financial data, or the disruption of financial markets).

The most important characteristic of cybercrime has now become not so much that of the innovation of the means, used to carry out the criminal offense, but more that of being branched into a transnational dimension, being equipped with support structures and connection, which allow links and solidarity between criminal subjects of different countries.

Computer crimes, understood as transnational crimes, due to their structural characteristics, presuppose a mobility of goods, services, things or people, between several States, or the use of the Internet, a communication tool capable of simultaneously breaking down space distances. - temporal and delocalizing and overturning the penal paradigms of the time and space, a physical place in which the criminal action may have been committed or attempted.

Ultimately, it cannot leave us indifferent that this enormous wealth escapes any form of taxation, causing, among other damages, even that of large-scale tax evasion with a conspicuous loss for public finance. Such cross-border criminal activities must therefore be effectively combated internationally so that the globalization process can continue smoothly.

Low risk, high return

Cybercrime is increasingly the object of interest and means of financing of large criminal organizations. This is due to a number of reasons, which will soon be presented.

Compared to crimes, which are committed in the real world, those of a virtual matrix, which are committed in cyberspace, consist of activities that are more easily achievable, which require few resources compared to the potential profit or harm caused. Among the virtual characteristics of the offense, it is, moreover, possible to enumerate: the immateriality, to territoriality and the high potential of offensive conduct, the high speed, the strong abstraction and the easy concealment of computer data, depersonalization and the consequent anonymity of the offender-victim confrontation, the possibility for the perpetrator of the crime to disappear and reappear under other guises in the virtual world, leaving traces that can only be decoded following intense investigations and international cooperation.

The cybergroups, which operate in the transnational network par excellence, have peculiar characteristics, such as flexibility and a high level of organization, which contribute to complicating the work of the investigative authorities and of all those bodies and institutions, which seek to prevent and to combat computer crimes. The aforementioned groups tend to maximize the opportunities offered by new communication technologies, information management and profits (possibility of crime and opportunities for enrichment) and to minimize the risk of being identified, arrested, convicted and having the proceeds of their criminal activities. These two factors change extremely rapidly as a function of variables that are difficult to manage, especially if their evaluation must be carried out on large and complex international scenarios.

If the economic implications can be extremely significant, the obstacles to judicial prosecution, linked to anonymity, in which communications take place and, above all, to the separation between the physical world and the virtual world, are certainly not insignificant. The scarce homogeneity of criminal legislation also contributes to making the real prosecution of cybercrime even more complex, due to which the same conduct can assume, depending on the legal system considered, different qualifications.

With deterritorialization, as a dimension that characterizes cyberspace, activities are not always precisely localizable. Individuals, groups and communities occupy, for the most diverse purposes, virtually a point of the network and, on the other hand, each terminal is able to reach it, through the address, which allows access. Said another way, the Internet knows no boundaries, not even those territorial boundaries, demarcating the legal systems.

CYBERSECURITY AND CYBERWAR
IN 2021

While the pervasiveness of information and communication technologies in modern societies has contributed to improving the performance of economic and civil systems, on the other hand it has exposed democracies to a relatively new type of crime, cybercrime, which in in recent years it has affected companies, public administrations, critical infrastructures and private users, causing large-scale damage. This new criminal form was born, grew and rooted simultaneously with the development of the Internet.

This is a criminal manifestation, which is not limited to national borders, but assumes, as demonstrated, a transnational connotation, which guarantees the agents a context of virtual impunity. Given the contradictory and heterogeneous international legal framework, the concern is that many states become potential gray zones, from which cybercriminals could operate without an adequate state response in terms of prevention, sanctioning, containment and enforcement.

Fighting such a phenomenon becomes a particularly complex operation, due to the jurisdictional problems that arise at national and international level. The traditional forms of jurisdiction, in fact, are based on the concept of "border" and the laws on that of territorial sovereignty. In cases of a cybercrime, having a transnational scope, the identification of the locus commissi delicti is very difficult. This entails the disappearance of a fundamental element of the criminal system of most legal systems, which are based on the principle of territoriality as the main criterion in the definition of the judge competent to know the illegal fact.

Considering that cybercrime has branched into a transnational dimension, we understand how it is necessary that the struggle to combat this phenomenon takes on the same character; this requires first of all the circulation of information and greater cooperation between the investigative authorities of the individual countries. Therefore, a transnational response is necessary for a phenomenon characterized by a transnational ramification, so that the globalization process can proceed smoothly. Therefore, it becomes imperative to prepare strategies, such as judicial collaboration and to have a common regulatory system as necessary prerequisites to counter this type of criminal manifestation. In such a complex context, it is necessary to abandon the purely nationalistic perspective of the repression of cybercrime, in favor of a universalistic approach, which goes beyond national limits in the implementation of the law.

The so-called "globalization of crime" therefore requires a "globalization of justice", to meet reasons of internal and international public security and with the specific aim of putting legal operators in the real conditions of repressing transnational cybercrime.

THE FUTURE OF CYBERSECURITY

Open systems, the growing connection between devices and sensors, data sensitivity and so on, are all variables that will make a big difference not only for manufacturers, but also for end users in the new year.

With a more open and connected environment, cyber risks and the need to protect sensitive data increase. For this reason, SIA's 2019 Security Megatrend puts the impact of cyber security on the physical security industry at the top of the list.

In fact, cyber security is increasingly involving every area of the industrial landscape, implementing new security systems in every sector of the economy, and launching itself in search of the best talents for the workforce in the sector.

Digital transformation

The digital transformation we are experiencing also impacts many other parts of the security industry, offering multiple opportunities.

At this critical time for industry development, it's important to embrace change by leveraging disruptive technology to give companies a competitive edge.

CYBERSECURITY AND CYBERWAR IN 2021

To determine the 2019 cybersecurity trends, SIA interviewed hundreds of executives of the associated companies, in order to identify the trends that are still relevant, those no longer impactful and the new ones to be added to the report.

Cyber security trends 2019

The 2019 cybersecurity trends can be traced back to 10 points that each company should consider:

- Impact of Cyber security on physical security:

- The company must give priority to IT security so as to protect not only its business, but also that of customers and suppliers.

- This requires continuous improvement of processes and investments.

- Internet of Things (IoT) and Big Data Effect: the security industry now makes use of IoT, analytics, artificial intelligence (AI), robotics and much more. Thousands of data come from all over the place. The industry now faces the challenge of effectively managing and segmenting this information.

- Cloud computing: cloud platforms and applications are becoming more and more important in security solutions.

- Workforce development:

- The search for qualified personnel is a challenge for the entire security sector. There is a continuing need for talented IT, cyber security, artificial intelligence, and even privacy expertise.

- Artificial intelligence: the research firm Gartner foresees a "democratization of AI" that will impact many more realities than in the past. Companies are testing this technology before offering it to customers, looking at how to use artificial intelligence data to improve cyber threat assessment and response.

- Emphasis on data privacy:

- Finding the balance between safety and convenience is a dilemma facing the industry now.

- Switch to service templates: the latest home security technologies are becoming in high demand. Businesses in the field need to focus on the services their customers want, and then move to better managed service models to maximize revenue.

- Integrated security in smart environments: everything becomes connected and smart environments begin to proliferate. Buildings and cities are becoming more aware, with connected systems now able to automatically respond and even anticipate the needs of users, infrastructure and citizens.

- We must continue to find ways to make these environments smarter and safer.

CYBERSECURITY AND CYBERWAR IN 2021

- Identity of the future: with facial and voice recognition and biometrics functions growing in popularity and appeal, how will we get into buildings and access networks in the future? Industry must anticipate and adapt to constant technological change.

- Impact of consumer electronics companies: the influx of consumer electronics and do-it-yourself systems companies is causing the rules and players in the security sector to change.

-As the years go by, we see the consequences of this arms race in the form of data breaches, malware outbreaks, privacy breaches and other compromising scenarios that ultimately affect customers, both consumers and businesses. These events continue to make headlines and, rightfully so, divert public attention to the importance of cybersecurity in our increasingly connected world.

Six F-Secure experts shared their predictions on what to expect in the near future. From IoT to AI, from security trends for organizations to consumer concerns, here are the trends that experts say will affect the near future.

The IoT will continue to grow and attract more interest from attackers

It's no secret that internet-connected devices, particularly Internet of Things (IoT) devices, are spreading like wildfire. We see more and more homes with connected thermostats, lights, voice assistants and entertainment systems.

For years, experts have been warning of IoT device security flaws - flaws that have led hackers to spy through home webcams, malware-infected IoT devices used to initiate DDoS attacks or other botnet-related activities.

"We have seen that these devices have been exploited, due to simple poor password policies, for remote code executions, up to DNS rebinding attacks," says Kankaala.

According to Kankaala, we will see more exploitation of these devices. But on the other hand, he hopes that increased exploitation will lead to regulation to stem the problem.

Attacks on the supply chain will increase

A supply chain attack is typically considered an attack that exploits the vulnerable parts of a supply network to target an organization. One of the best-known examples is perhaps the 2017 NotPetya ransomware attack, when an update of Ukrainian tax accounting software was compromised and used to run malware rather than an actual update. The attack unfortunately caused a billion of dollars in losses and affected not only Ukrainian businesses but also spread to major organizations around the world.

But Artturi Lehtio, F-Secure Service Technology, points out that supply chain attacks are incredibly diverse and can even affect individuals.

CYBERSECURITY AND CYBERWAR IN 2021

"We are putting much of our life in the hands of others, and we don't always realize how much we rely on others or on the trust of others. We really have no way of verifying whether they are still worthy of that trust," explains Lehtio.

The Infostealer will aim to users' devices to maximize the profit of the attacks

There have been three main types of malware hitting users last year: Cryptominers, which harness the computing power of a device to secretly mine cryptocurrency; banking Trojans, which infect a victim's device and then search for the victim's bank details.

Christine Bejerasco, Vice President, Tactical Defense UnitSecurity Research & Technologies, says all three will continue to be used this year, but in collaboration with the infostealers that the malware authors have begun to use to target the device before hitting it with the actual payload.

"Last year, there was an increase in cryptominers which coincided with the increase in valuations of cryptocurrencies," Bejerasco explains. "Then, as cryptocurrency ratings started to drop, malware writers started to become more opportunistic, putting an infostealer on a user's device to figure out if they could earn more by then inserting a cryptominer, banking trojan or ransomware. on the victim's car. This trend will continue. "

CYBERSECURITY AND CYBERWAR IN 2021

PUBLIC WI-FI WILL CONTINUE TO BE DANGEROUS

But does the fact that more and more websites are encrypted, with "https" to ensure visitors their data is safe, mean it's time to ease concerns about public Wi-Fi security? In my opinion the answer is no.

Even as people are using websites that increasingly encrypt their traffic and implement certificates correctly, there is still a combination of certificate theft and profiling via DNS traffic that can potentially compromise a user.

To me, anyone using public Wi-Fi should secure their connection using a VPN, while also blocking third-party tracking by advertisers.

Contrary to the catastrophic messages we often hear, Tom Van de Wiele, Principal Security Consultant at F-Secure, believes we can expect positive security developments in the near future.

"We see a definite trend of customers introducing more and more software and services," explains Tom.

Breaches will continue to expose customer data

Data breaches, which regularly make headlines, affect not only businesses but also the customers they serve, who must therefore take precautions to prevent or mitigate identity theft.

CYBERSECURITY AND CYBERWAR

IN 2021

"The number of hacked businesses continues to increase, with user data being pulled and sold," says Bejerasco, who doesn't expect breaches to slow down in the short term. There's not much a consumer can do to affect the internal security position of the companies they support in any way, but there are other ways to protect your data, says Bejerasco. "Be careful which websites you enter your information and credentials on," he says. "Even if the site is legitimate, if it doesn't have a strict cybersecurity process, compromising it could be cheap and easy and that means the data you provided could be breached."

Organizations will start thinking about why they could be hacked

Adam Sheehan, Behavioral Science Lead at MWR Infosecurity, studies the social engineering tactics used by attackers to trick people into clicking and how people respond to those tactics. Sheehan predicts that more companies will start to be interested in what she describes as the next level of analysis - not just what risky behaviors their employees engage in.

"I think for too long it has been assumed that if organization A has a high click-through rate, say on phishing emails, and organization B has the same high click-through rate seen on phishing emails, then it should be offered, more or less the same solution," says Adam. "Actually, in one case the underlying issue could be a certain problem. And in the other, the underlying problem may be quite different."

Sheehan says this desire among companies to go deeper into root cause analysis will grow and push organizations to seek tailored solutions to address the problem their particular organizations frontline.

Privacy issues will continue to affect users

Snowden's 2013 revelations, when government whistleblower and contractor Edward Snowden exposed the government's global surveillance programs to the public, brought privacy concerns to the fore. Almost six years later, privacy concerns still plague cyberspace and users should still be aware of themselves and how their data is used and shared by organizations, apps and services, says Bejerasco, starting with mobile devices.

"On mobile devices, be careful about the permissions you grant to the apps you install," he says. "Some of them may be capturing behavioral data, and their systems are then able to create profiles of your behavior that owners can use or sell to others. Always make sure to only provide permissions that support the features you need from that app. "

Reinforcement learning will continue to take a big leap forward

One example is how it can be used to teach a computer to play a car racing video game - after enough repetition, the computer would learn for itself how to press the accelerator, the brakes and turn the wheel to avoid an accident.

"There are many other similar applications in cybersecurity, especially with regards to penetration testing or fuzzing which are interesting. Like guessing the password, or application fuzzing, stuff like that. So, I guess you could actually publish - even if it's just academic - something that uses reinforcement learning for this kind of thing. "

Cybersecurity awareness in the school world

Those who work in the field of IT security are well aware of the importance of infosharing and dissemination. The school is the main place to start from to increase the culture of security, but the specialized training for teachers and the management of the cyber environment in schools cannot be left to the goodwill of the professionals, teachers and auxiliary staff. .

The school as a reference point for education and culture, an obviousness in relation to standard curricular subjects, which ceases to be obvious as soon as we talk about computer security as a subject to be disclosed among children for the risks that can affect them on the Net (luring and scams), for the problems related to cyberbullying and for the necessary elimination of the digital divide.

Some professionals in the world of cybersecurity are engaged at the forefront in the activities of dissemination and dissemination of knowledge on the issues of information security, precisely to make up for the chronic lack of organization, resources and means that afflicts the school world. But this voluntary commitment does not constitute a systematic solution, nor can it be sufficient.

Microsoft is committed to this work of awareness throughout the country, also by virtue of the recent cyber-attacks suffered by the world of education, to inform and disseminate security and data protection issues to school operators. The aim is to train school operators on the right behaviors and on the technologies to be implemented for data security on the Net, on how to create awareness among students, on the dangers of the digital world and on the countermeasures to be adopted to mitigate risks.

Start with an overview of the risks and major security incidents to understand the threat landscape, and focus on the importance and risks of digital data. Teachers and managerial staff were impressed and concerned by the finding that the school is one of the realities with the highest data rate in an absolute sense and with the least control in terms of processes and organization and management. This type of information events should also be organized for children and families, although declined in a different way. It is also necessary to give indications on what to do, even if a cultural problem arises on the knowledge of the ICT technology to be managed. It would be necessary to create the conditions for informing and teaching both technology and the implications of security by making those who then have to educate children understand the risks in the use of digital tools.

Here we see an interview from an internationally renowned cybersecurity whose name we will not give the name for privacy reasons:

What conditions did you find from the point of view of security and operational countermeasures?

I explained the importance of the "Lead by example" which is valid in Microsoft but which represents a good general practice. Basically, I made it clear to the teaching staff that they must be credible on certain issues, just as they already do on other issues: some institutes carry out projects such as the one related to a device that allows you to control an Android smartphone using only the movement of the head, but three big data startups have also been launched. Of course, they are happy islands, but unfortunately, they do not represent a custom. The teaching staff must absorb the considerations we have shared and then not turn to the other side, but act and not only on the data but also on access to data, on the management of the entire school information system. And here the problems arise: they are not people dedicated to the PC park, to the management and administration of the network. There are willing people who try to help. In the institute, the electronic register used in the cloud is currently used, and essentially represents a black box because it does not share data with the institute's systems since everything is managed via the web. Furthermore, the institute already uses the Microsoft office 365 platform and therefore a sort of compliance exists because it is given by the product, but certainly there could be processing of data exchanged via email that may be out of control and not compliant.

How can the school work to prepare the appropriate countermeasures?

During the meeting I suggested simple actions, which can constitute an initial phase: create a committee in the school in which people with skills on technological, security and data protection issues become owners of an internal activity, aimed at creating an infrastructure local authentication to implement controlled access (using username and password associated with individual users by verifying their identity and authorization), or even through cloud services, to create a user database, with appropriate profiling (authorization configuration) according to the type of user. It is necessary to implement a perimeter defense and also in this case the cloud could be of help, since in the presence of a PC fleet it is possible to connect the devices on the network also guaranteeing the management of endpoints. For the post there are tools natively designed for the education sector. A simplified model of this type, after a first implementation in one school as a pilot project, could be replicated in other institutions. But at least a path should begin: volunteering is not enough, but it can be a starting point. After it would be necessary to have a program, strategies, at the ministry level and at the local level, concrete resources would be needed.

Do we need an institutional commitment in this sense?

Digitization does not seem a priority of political programs, although there is a digital agenda and innovation plan for the UK. It seems that the big programs are struggling to permeate the local reality. In schools we see manifestations of goodwill and although in terms of teaching quality we are still among the best, the digital tools and the organization for the management and teaching of information security for data protection, must improve with targeted investments because it is in the schools that begin the process of creating a culture.

How is the situation in the universities?

I recently gave a webinar for universities on the same topic. It is interesting to note the difference between universities and schools from primary to high school. The differentiating element concerns the presence of ICT infrastructures in universities, with dedicated people. Awareness on the issues of security and data protection is greater as is the knowledge of the legislation. If we want, we could say that in universities there is a "problem for the rich", that is, there is already a solid basis on which to carry out improvements and optimization interventions, such as the definition of the profiling of the user groups, in the face of an already present identity management. Or an improvement could be the evolution towards cloud platforms by adopting the shared responsibility model between them and the Cloud Provider.

Does security represent a "management of the rich" for what it has seen between school and university, or can only those entities that have certain economic conditions afford it?

I wouldn't say that's correct, safety comes from culture, competence and infrastructure. Doing it and doing it well is a further step but it depends on the type of risk you want to manage. For everything else you can resort to outsourcing. In school, the main asset is children, and their data must be protected in a way that is effective. Certainly, resources, including economic ones, are needed to do this.

What are the goals of cybersecurity?

The term "Cyber Security" has now become famous through the multitude of films, set in the new millennium, in which technological threats often reveal themselves as the weapons of the new generation.

Yet it is not easy to understand the objectives and the importance of this term which has landed in everyday reality and in our own language, but of which we often know very little.

CYBERSECURITY AND CYBERWAR
IN 2021

In the course of this book, we will therefore discover what the objectives of cyber security are and which tools are used to ensure maximum effectiveness.

What are the tools adopted to achieve the objectives of IT security?

Cyber security has as its main objective the protection of "assets" such as a site, a computer or a car, against cyber threats, and at the same time tries to minimize the impact in the case of vulnerabilities that exceed the defenses implemented.

This turns out to be a difficult task, and it is therefore necessary to introduce some specific points to be met so that it is possible to develop effective policies and procedures to prevent part of the risks from turning into threats.

What is the "CIA Triad"?

The specific points mentioned above are grouped within the "CIA Triad", also called "AIC" to avoid confusion with the famous "Central Intelligence Agency".

"AIC" is the acronym formed by the initials of the 3 pillars on which Cyber Security rests, namely " Availability ", " Confidentiality " and " Integrity ".

The fact that both names can be used without any difference is linked to the fact that there is no more important factor as they all contribute to objectively define the severity of the threat. They are in fact the basis of the system for identifying the severity of a vulnerability, or the "CVSS score".

Going more specifically, the various terms take on important connotations:

Confidentiality: not intended simply as avoiding the dissemination of private information, but also allowing access to such information only to those who are authorized and denying it to those who are not, or making it possible for its use only to the originally designated persons;

Integrity: that is, preserving the truthfulness of information and making sure that it is real and accurate, as well as protected against unauthorized changes;

Availability: i.e. the ownership of the service to manage and operate efficiently and continuously, without interruptions.

Recently it was also decided to introduce the concept of "Privacy" into the triad: it could take on a different meaning compared to Confidentiality following the numerous violations concerning the conservation and dissemination of our data.

What are the tools adopted to achieve the objectives of IT security?

On the basis of the principle to be satisfied, there are tools that make it possible to guarantee the application of the

3 factors and to minimize the risk of threats that can seriously compromise a company's IT security.

For confidentiality:

- Use of encryption systems in order to make the information unreadable by anyone not authorized to access it;

- Access controls, that is the set of rules and procedures adopted to limit access to a system or resource

- Authentication, a process that allows the identification of the user;

- For integrity:

- Backup, i.e. the process of periodic file copying which is particularly useful in the event of data loss or destruction;

- Checksum, i.e. the assignment of a numerical value calculated through an algorithm that allows to validate that the file has not been modified in the time since the last check carried out.

For availability:

- Physical protections consisting of different methods to keep the system operational, preventing power outages and more or less serious damage to the hardware, in order to avoid service interruption;

- Web protections, i.e. defenses such as CDN and DNS in order to counter any DDOS attacks that could overload the server by putting the service out of use.

For anyone novice in the field of "Cyber Security", as well as for anyone with a blog, a recent car or simply a bank account, it is essential to fully understand what are the purposes towards which IT security and its importance.

In fact, never before have cyber threats put our information at risk and invite us to pay attention to the risks we run and the solutions we have.

THE CYBER RISKS TO BE ADDRESSED IN 2020

Cyber risks increase as technology environments become more complicated and legacy systems and data centers, public cloud services and SaaS applications spread. What are the trends and threats that will characterize the coming months?

In 2020, the main vectors of cyber risk will continue to be emails and applications open to the Internet. According to experts, email-borne computer viruses evolve rapidly and hackers find new ways every day to evade traditional security solutions. Each company will therefore have to equip itself with more advanced protection systems in line with the evolution of IT risks and cyber-attacks, also followed by external professionals able to offer advice for the implementation of the protection measures of information systems.

An insurance broker follows the company from the risk analysis to the selection of the optimal cyber policy.

Cyber Security

Our professionals accompany organizations to implement an efficient IT security system.

Cloud, SaaS applications, brute force attacks

The biggest threat expected in 2020 is largely new.

Switching to "serverless" does not solve the security problems. Still, web application security is often overlooked because most organizations lack the skills or resources to manage these solutions. In addition, many businesses assume that the necessary protection is provided by their hosting service, which however hardly offers adequate coverage. The trend towards cloud- based and as -a-service application security solutions can help make security more accessible for more organizations and address the problem for years to come.

For these largely unaddressed critical issues, cloud-based collaboration and production software are among the targets of choice for hackers.

Phishing via Email

Interception of conversations, spoofing of people's voices and highly targeted attacks will make business email compromise (BEC) attacks even more convincing. The spear phishing easily draws in deception, being targeted to only one person, most of the so-called spray phishing, mass attack that tries to involve as many victims as possible and is less personal and credible. Recent research by IT solutions company Barracuda finds that BEC accounts for only 7% of spear phishing attacks, but the cost of a successful attack can be very high. According to the FBI, companies have lost $26 billion to BEC attacks over the past 4 years, and the figure is likely to grow rapidly thanks to new criminal tactics. Furthermore, the more hackers find ways to exploit vulnerabilities, the more targeted attacks on the IoT will develop.

Complex infection processes

In 2019, most email attacks relied on malicious URLs to deliver malware, not attachments. Cybercriminals will exploit these evolutions, both because of the effectiveness of social engineering techniques and because URLs can mask infection processes that are even more difficult to detect.

Ransomware

They are not the most used, but ransomware made headlines in 2019 and will continue to be so in 2020. They mainly aim at high-ransom operations to unlock servers and endpoints, but they will play a secondary role compared to infections using Trojans and RATs (Remote Access Trojan), malware inside genuine programs, downloaders and banking Trojans, making prevention and defense essential. Businesses will understand that being hit by ransomware means they have already been compromised by a host of malware that create future vulnerabilities and expose you to the risk of data and intellectual property loss.

Privacy and compliance with the GDPR

In 2020, Chief Information Security Officers (CISOs), responsible for corporate cyber security, will need to be fully aware of the proliferation of privacy and compliance laws being implemented around the world. The GDPR is just the beginning: we need to be ready to adapt to the introduction of similar regulations, with enormous and increasingly complex implications, especially for companies operating on an international scale. CISOs will also need to be effective in finding the support of the CEO and senior managers for safety-related initiatives: it will be essential to clearly communicate safety-related issues to obtain the necessary resources to face new challenges. It will be increasingly important for security managers to focus on how to integrate security into the corporate culture so that everyone within the organization is aware of the role they play in keeping the company safe.

CYBERSECURITY AND CYBERWAR IN 2021

Sectors targeted by cyber criminals

The favorite targets of hackers and cybercriminals will continue to be small businesses and schools. These industries often operate with low budgets, minimal security measures, outdated technologies, and a small IT staff - the ideal ground for a wide range of attacks, such as ransomware.

Cybercriminals seek to target areas where returns are highest: The latest trends in email security indicate that they are looking for new ways to accumulate money by targeting business email compromise (ECB) attacks. Such attacks lead the end user to make payments directly rather than stealing information. Attacks by foreign powers will also intensify, aimed at targeting the intellectual properties of industries of strategic importance to states, those of the aerospace, defense, technology, manufacturing and pharmaceutical sectors, or structures where they can cause serious damage, such as utilities and transport.

Over the past two years, we have seen direct and targeted attacks on power plants around the world. The criminal operations used ransomware undetectable by normal Anti-Malware systems. Detecting and addressing these attacks, aimed at gaining access to credentials for Industrial Control Systems (ICS) and Supervisory Control and Data Acquisition Systems (SCADA), is vital for businesses that want to avoid widespread consequences including disruption of local power plants and energy supplies.

CYBERSECURITY AND CYBERWAR IN 2021

Consequences on the company organization

Technological environments become complicated every year: companies continue to manage legacy systems and data centers, the 5 G network spreads, which promises to connect almost all aspects of daily life across the network with unmatched speed. Each news in the IT field implies new challenges to ensure the highest possible degree of security. In fact, unprecedented access points are born that expose companies to new types of attacks. All of this has implications for both security teams and the managers who run businesses. IT teams need to monitor more attack points. Many CEOs expect the company to evolve, but are reluctant to allocate resources to the IT team to keep up with the increased security that development demands. In 2020, companies will increasingly have to rely on effective use of technology and automation to solve the gaps between budget and development needs.

Training must be a core asset

Automated systems can protect inboxes from many threats, but users are the final line of defense, especially when it comes to voice and SMS phishing (smishing). Consequently, training is an essential component of safety. It is expected that in 2020:

- training priorities will be indicated by threat intelligence and the type of threats suffered;

- companies will rely on users' abilities to identify possible phishing attacks and on automated reporting activities;

- companies will focus on training and training dedicated to internal phishing and compromising email accounts, which are complicated to detect with automatic systems.

An extended cyber risk

Supply chain vulnerabilities were at the center of attacks on major retailers in 2013 and 2014. All this will bring the IT security skill gap beyond a bearable threshold in terms of business risk. Handling the problem in an inadequate manner risks having excessive impacts on business continuity and company profits.

According to some data provided by Symantec, 68% of adults have been victims of online crimes. However, cybercrime is not a legally defined category, nor is there an internationally recognized definition of "computer crime" or "cybercrime".

Cyber security is now a strategic element to ensure the economic and social prosperity of a country. In fact, the ever faster and more intense development of information and communication technologies is accompanied by the equally rapid and widespread diffusion of new criminal forms, which can be grouped in the category of cybercrime, and which evolve much more rapidly than legal solutions. necessary to solve the problems that arise. Just think of the actions carried out by terrorist groups increasingly based on new technologies, the continuous development of networks linked to pornography or pedophilia, the illicit trafficking of weapons, drugs, human beings, dirty money. In addition to these global problems, more than a million individuals are victims of cybercrime every day. To this are added other actions that anyone, even unwittingly, can now perform.

According to some data provided by Symantec, out of a sample of 24 countries, 44% of adults were victims of online crimes, compared to 15% of adults victims of offline crimes, while in Italy the percentage of cybercrime victims rises to 68%. . However, cybercrime does not consist of a legally defined category, even though it appears in European and supranational sources. Similarly, there is no internationally recognized definition of "computer crime" or "computer related crime" or "cybercrime". However, it is certain that there is a cyberspace, that is, a virtual space that allows the relocation of resources and their reachability by the user from any place and distance, also thanks to the new dimension of cloud computing. This is accompanied by the detemporalization of activities, which can be planned and carried out through automated operations programmed by the user, without the need for his physical presence on the computer. Therefore, the Internet and the new communication and information technologies have criminogenic potential while the phenomenon of cybercrime is flexible and open to criminal acts that can be committed through the network or in cyberspace.

Referring to the American doctrine, three sub-categories can be included in the cybercrime category:

- ❖ crimes in which the computer or computer system is the target of criminal activities;
- ❖ crimes in which the computer, new technologies and the Internet represent the tools for committing or preparing a crime;
- ❖ Crimes in which the computer system and the network constitute only an "incidental aspect" in the commission of the offense.

The Council of Europe Convention on Cybercrime, signed in Budapest on November 23, 2001 and entered into force in July 2004, is the only binding international treaty existing today on this issue. The treaty establishes guidelines for all states wishing to develop comprehensive national legislation against cybercrime and identifies some cybercrime:

- ❖ Illegal access to a computer system
- ❖ Abusive interception
- ❖ Attack on data integrity
- ❖ Attack on the integrity of a system
- ❖ Abuse of equipment

- Computer forgery
- Computer fraud
- Crimes relating to child pornography
- Crimes against intellectual property

Attention to the phenomenon is growing and, in Europe, with the entry into force of the Lisbon Treaty, cybercrime has been included in art. 83 of the Treaty on the Functioning of the European Union, among the criminal phenomena of a serious and transnational nature over which the European Union has criminal jurisdiction. In addition to the phenomena that have been known for years, there are many threats that are developing and making the phenomenon of cybercrime more insidious. In fact, the development of mobile computing also means the development of mobile cybercrime, which translates into a risk for transactions and payments via mobile devices, phishing on mobile devices (vishing and smishing) and fraudulent mobile applications.

Added to this is the growing use of personal systems to access sensitive corporate data (Byod - Bring Your Own Device), which presents the risk of breaching corporate systems through employees' personal devices. On the other hand, companies will also be increasingly subjected to attacks on the cloud or through the cloud.

Still, the creation of financial banking trojans and malware undoubtedly persists, where personal additions are made to traditional malware, with the typical use of the

English language but with an increase in the use of the Russian language.

Then, account theft and manual cyberattack continue, but traditional man-in-the-browser Trojan attacks are accompanied by an increasing use of man-in-the-middle Trojan attacks, that is, where there is physical presence. of an operator to conduct the cyber-attack.

The same cyber-attacks are improving their effectiveness thanks to data filtering and data charting and, therefore, the development of more sophisticated malware models thanks to data analytics, while the incremental use of social networks can be a further vector of increasingly more cyber-attacks personalized (social networking feeds).

In addition to all this, the phenomenon of hacktivism is growing, that is, of cyber-attacks for ideological, social, political reasons, etc. Although seen as forms of ideological protest or the public expression of controversial social and political opinions, the phenomenon presents increasing risks given the advent of hacktivist groups and the development of links between hacktivists and cybercriminals motivated by economic purposes.

Finally, the new frontier of cyber-attacks reaches space and can involve the International Space Station, satellites and other space infrastructures that are now indispensable for daily life, such as weather forecasts, satellite television channels, synchronization of banking operations, the transmission of trading operations, air, sea and land navigation, the GPS of military operations.

CYBERSECURITY AND CYBERWAR IN 2021

In consideration of the transnational scope of cybercrime, various forms of formal and informal cooperation between states have developed, through regional mechanisms (Council of Europe Convention on Cybercrime, Convention of the League of Arab States, etc.) and networks (Interpol, Europol, G8, NATO Cooperative Cyber Defense Center of Excellence, etc.).

However, beyond the scenarios outlined, cybercrime is really very close to each of us: just remember the crimes against intellectual property that are committed every day by ordinary people, even simply by downloading a movie from the web. In fact, on March 31, 2014 the Authority for Guarantees in Communications (AGCOM) issued a regulation for online copyright, the first initiative aimed at addressing online piracy (and radio and television) in an administrative way and counteracting the availability of digital works in violation of the copyright of the owners.

The new procedure allows you to order the selective removal of content in violation of copyright and the disabling of access to said content. Clearly all this opens up scenarios that are difficult to predict, especially with regard to the application, by AGCOM, of the principles of graduality, proportionality and adequacy.

For example, since it is possible to resort to an abbreviated emergency procedure (thanks to which the procedure ends in 12 days instead of the 35 otherwise provided for by the standard procedure), the violation relating to a film showing at that moment in theaters could

CYBERSECURITY AND CYBERWAR IN 2021

be considered worthy of greater protection than the violation relating to a film of sometime before? The picture outlined so far is certainly not exhaustive, yet it offers a varied panorama of the threats that cybercrime poses to individuals, companies and entire countries, at the same time highlighting the need to define a cybersecurity strategy that also needs to be beyond national borders.

www.ingramcontent.com/pod-product-compliance
Lightning Source LLC
Chambersburg PA
CBHW060829220526
45466CB00003B/1037